fabulous
CAKE DECORATING
Step-by-Step Instruction for Beautiful Results

BETTERWAY BOOKS
CINCINNATI, OHIO

Front and back cover photographs and spine: Eaglemoss Publications Ltd/Sue Atkinson
Title page: Eaglemoss Publications Ltd/Tif Hunter
Page 4: Eaglemoss Publications Ltd/Sue Atkinson

Produced by Eaglemoss Publications
Based on *Creative Hands, Country Look* and *Creative Cook*
Copyright © Eaglemoss Publications Ltd 2000

First published in North America
in 2000 by Betterway Books
an imprint of F&W Publications, Inc
1507 Dana Avenue
Cincinnati, Ohio 45207
1-800/289-0963

ISBN 1-55870-549-X

Printed and bound in Spain by Bookprint, S.L, Barcelona

10 9 8 7 6 5 4 3 2 1

CONTENTS

1

VERSATILE ICING

2

IDEAS FOR SPECIAL OCCASIONS

1
VERSATILE ICING

Introducing cake decoration

The art of cake decorating has flourished over the last decade, with the result that ingredients and accessories are now readily available. A marzipan covering is the first step in decorating any formal fruit cake, and the same principles can be used to add a covering of sugarpaste.

Marzipan and sugarpaste are available commercially from supermarkets and grocery stores.

Marzipan is most often used to cover rich fruit cakes, before finishing with crisp royal icing. It can also be used as a decoration in its own right: simnel cake, with simple balls of marzipan topped with a dusting of cinnamon is a traditional Lenten cake.

Sugarpaste can be used as a decorative covering on top of the marzipan and can be moulded into slightly more delicate shapes. It dries harder than marzipan.

Materials and equipment
Marzipan
Marzipan is a paste made from ground almonds and sugar and is available ready-made. To obtain the best results always use fresh, pliable marzipan and keep it moist by wrapping it in foil.

White marzipan should be used whenever possible as it is ideal for modelling work and can be easily tinted.

Yellow marzipan tends to show through thin icing and, as it already contains food colouring, is much harder to tint. It is useful for modelling marzipan fruits, and for decorating cakes where a yellow background is required.

Raw sugar marzipan is a dark brown paste. It is available from most health shops.

Sugarpaste

Sugarpaste or cake fondant icing is a stiff icing which is used as a decorative covering on cakes or to sculpt a wide range of decorations and models, such as flowers, fruit and animals.

It can be made using a variety of recipes (for example, fondant or gelatine icing) or bought ready-made. Different brands vary in pliability, so try it out before buying a large amount. Knead the paste well before starting to work it. Keep the sugarpaste fresh in a polythene bag while you are working.

Colourants

It is worth keeping a good stock of colours, so that you can mix them to create the shade you are after. When colouring icing, always tint more than you think you will need, as it is difficult to match colours if you run out. Most colourants contain chemicals to which some children may be allergic.

Paste is probably the most versatile colourant and only a small amount is needed to create bright, vibrant colours. It can be kneaded into the icing, or thinned with water and painted on the surface. Paste can be bought from supermarkets or specialist shops.

Liquid colour can be used in the same way as paste, and is more readily available, but tends to soften the material being tinted. It is not as concentrated as paste and therefore produces subtle pastel shades.

Sugarpaste pens and powder are also used for colouring icing.

Tools

A small sharp kitchen knife, skewers or cocktail sticks, a rolling pin, a pastry brush and pastry cutters are the main kitchen utensils you need to make the decorations shown in this chapter. A child's rolling pin is useful for rolling small amounts of icing.

You can also buy special tools for adding patterns to cakes, and shapes, such as crimpers, which are used to 'punch' a pattern on to the surface of the icing. Cake boards covered in decorative foil will give a professional look to a decorated cake.

Covering round and square cakes

The foundation of good cake decoration is a covering of smooth marzipan, either as a finish itself or as a base for further layers of icing.

Use the marzipan generously. In order to get a smooth finish, it has to fill the unevenness of the surface of the cake beneath. Sprinkle confectioner's sugar over the surface and knead the marzipan well before you start. Sugarpaste is applied over a base of marzipan, and is handled in much the same way. Some people prefer to use cornflour when rolling out sugarpaste as this is finer than confectioner's sugar.

Either type of covering can be coloured before being applied, or decorated afterwards with simple coloured motifs or moulded shapes, for example. You can make these yourself or use bought decorations for a quick but effective finish.

Start by trimming the top of the cake, or flatten it with a rolling pin if the fruit makes lumps and bumps. It is usually easiest to use the flat bottom of the cake as the top, to ensure a good surface.

Covering a cake with marzipan

1 Apricot jam is used to help the marzipan stick in place. Heat up the jam and rub it through a sieve. Brush it on to the surface of the cake.

4 Use your hands to press the paste on to the surface of the cake, starting at the top and smoothing down the sides.

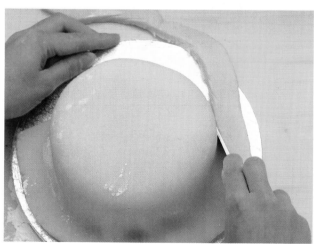

5 With a sharp knife, remove the excess paste from around the base of the cake.

Cutters

Child's rolling pin

Sugar paste

White marzipan

Yellow marzipan

Cake board

Paste colourant

Liquid colour

Crimpers

Cocktail sticks

Cornflour

Sharp knife

Using crimpers
For a simple decorative finish around the top of a cake, you can add a design using special crimpers. Simply pinch the icing with the crimpers, making sure you space the marks evenly.

2 Sprinkle a little confectioner's sugar on the work surface. Roll out the paste so that it is large enough to wrap right over the top of the cake.

3 Using your rolling pin to support the paste, so that it does not crack, gently lift the marzipan over the entire cake.

TIP   **SQUARE CORNERS**

For crisp corners, particularly on a square cake, cover the top with a separate piece of marzipan. Brush glaze on the top of the cake, then roll out the paste so that it is about 1in (2.5cm) larger all round than the top of the cake. Turn the cake upside down and place it centrally on the paste, then trim the marzipan in line with the edge of the cake.

Glaze the sides of the cake, then cut strips for the sides and press them in place.

To ensure the strips are the right length for the cake, use a piece of string to measure along each side (or around a circular cake). Cover the sides of the cake one at a time, so that the paste overlaps at each of the corners. Finally, use your fingers to smooth over the joins.

Tinting marzipan and sugar paste

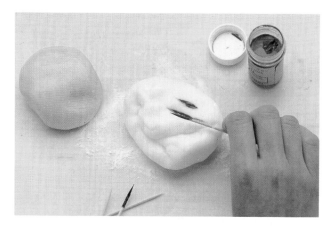

Use a skewer or cocktail stick to transfer tiny drops of paste or liquid colouring to the icing. Working on a surface covered in icing sugar, knead the colour into the paste to blend it in evenly.

Cutting shapes

Use a sharp knife for simple shapes, or small cutters for curved, crimped or star shapes. Roll the paste out to the required thickness, dip the knife or cutter in confectioner's sugar and press it into the paste.

Parcel cake

Whatever the occasion, this cake wrapped in marzipan is an appropriate centrepiece. Start with a ready-made cake, glazed and smoothly wrapped in yellow marzipan icing. It is better to use white marzipan (or sugarpaste icing) for the shapes, to give cleaner colours when you add the colourant.

You will need
◇ A square or round cake
◇ A cake board
◇ Apricot jam, sieve, saucepan and pastry brush
◇ Confectioner's sugar
◇ Yellow and white marzipan
◇ Blue, violet and green food colouring
◇ A sharp knife
◇ Small cutters
◇ Greaseproof paper

Tint and roll out the blue marzipan, then cut into strips to go over the cake. Measure and mark guidelines before positioning them.

Tint and roll out the violet and green paste. Cut out the shapes and arrange some so they look as though they are partly underneath the ribbon. Cut more strips of blue paste to form a bow, and support the loops with screwed up paper until the marzipan has dried out.

Making royal icing

*Satin smooth and brilliantly white, royal icing
is the traditional icing for formal cakes. With a little practice,
you can master the art of making this versatile
icing and with swirls, peaks and piping give your homemade cakes
a truly professional finish.*

12

Many experienced cake makers steer clear of making royal icing for fear of failure. But don't be put off! Royal icing is the covering used for the icing and decoration on wedding cakes and anniversary cakes. Unlike marzipan and sugarpaste, royal icing cannot be bought ready made, so you will need to find the best recipe for your purposes before you attempt to cover the cake and then decorate it.

Materials and equipment
All the equipment needed for royal icing should be scrupulously clean because if the cake is kept for any length of time, any bacteria will cause it to develop mould.

Cake boards
The board you put the cake on is part of the design as well, so choose carefully. Foil-covered cake boards are readily available in large supermarkets, bakers and stationers. You can cover the board yourself with patterned or coloured paper or fabric. Use a cornflour and water paste to glue the covering to the board.

Another way to decorate the board is to cover it with royal icing. This is done after the cake has been covered and is thoroughly dry. The board is then iced too and the piped designs can be continued on to the board following the same theme as the icing on the cake.

The board should be at least 1in (2.5cm) larger all round than the cake to give you room to work and to leave space for surface decoration and when cutting. Making tiered cakes and putting them on boards is covered in a later chapter.

Turntables
These are useful when working with royal icing as they give you freedom of movement. An upturned plate is adequate to raise the cake off the surface.

Levelling implements
A palette knife is used to smooth and trim the icing; a straight edge is for levelling the top of the cake; a side scraper smooths the sides of the cake and the board.

Other tools
Pillars are used to hold the boards in a tiered cake. A sieve for the confectioner's sugar is essential. To perfect the icing technique, there are polystyrene dummies available from cake decorating suppliers for you to practise on. You will also need glasspaper to sand any rough icing when dry and a brush to remove any powder after sanding.

Royal icing recipe
To make 1lb (500g) of icing, follow either of these recipes. Use good-quality confectioner's sugar and sieve it thoroughly to remove the lumps.

If you are following the recipe using egg whites, glycerine may be added to produce a slightly softer result. Royal icing when it is built up into a number of layers can be thick to cut. Glycerine will make the icing easier to cut. Add 1½-2tsp (8-10ml) glycerine to 1lb (500g) confectioner's sugar. Beat it in to the finished icing.

Do not add the glycerine if you are using the icing for fine piped designs.

You will need
◇ 2-3tsp (1015ml) powdered egg albumen
◇ 4tbsp (4 x 15ml spoons) water
◇ 1lb (500g) confectioner's sugar, sifted
OR
◇ 2-3 egg whites
◇ ¼tsp (1ml) lemon juice
◇ 1lb (500g) confectioner's sugar, sifted
◇ glycerine (optional)

Place the egg albumen and water in a large bowl. Whisk with a fork until well mixed. Alternatively, place egg whites and lemon juice in a bowl and whisk lightly.

Stir in sufficient sieved confectioner's sugar to make the consistency of unwhipped heavy cream. With a wooden spoon, beat in small quantities of confectioner's sugar until the mixture becomes very white and forms a peak on the spoon.

Cake boards / Sieve / Confectioner's sugar / Glass bowl / Turntable / Side scraper / Straight edge / Palette knife

| TIP | PERFECT ICING |

◇ Cover the icing in the bowl with a damp cloth during the time you are using it – any unused icing can be stored in an airtight container.
◇ Make small amounts of icing at a time so there is less risk of it spoiling.
◇ The icing for covering a cake should be less stiff than that used for piping.

Covering a cake

When applying royal icing to a marzipan-covered cake, the aim is to achieve a perfectly smooth finish. Take your time and allow each layer or section to dry before adding another.

You will need

◇ Royal icing (in a covered bowl)
◇ Marzipan-covered cake
◇ A palette knife
◇ A side scraper
◇ A straight edge or a new clean ruler
◇ Turntable or upturned plate
◇ Fine glasspaper over a sanding block
◇ A clean soft brush
◇ Clean damp cloth
◇ Boiling water in a bowl

1 Place the cake on a board and put it on a turntable or upturned plate and place a quantity of icing into the centre. Using a palette knife start to spread the icing thinly over the top making a 'paddling' motion. Place a bowl of boiling water to one side of your working space, and dip the palette knife into it from time to time to help the knife go smoothly over the surface.

2 Remove the excess icing from the top edges of the cake. Take the straight edge and steadily pull it across the top to give a final smooth surface. Neaten the edges with the palette knife once more before leaving the icing to dry for at least one hour.

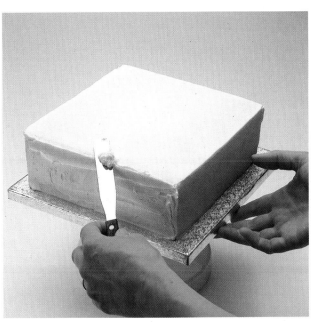

3 Spread the sides of the cake with the icing in the same way. For a square cake, ice the two opposite sides first, leave to dry and then ice the remaining two sides.

4 Take care to remove the surplus icing from edges and corners as each side is iced to form sharp corners.

5 Take the side scraper and place it at a slight angle to the side of the cake. Pull it towards you and take off the excess to smooth the sides. Leave it to dry overnight. Use the fine glasspaper on the sanding block to remove any roughness and brush off the powdered icing. Place any unused icing into an airtight container.

6 The cake will need two more coats of icing applied in the same way before it is ready for decorating. Spread a thin layer of icing on the board and pull the scraper along the edge to smooth it down. This provides a useful surface to continue the decoration.

Textured finishes

For less formal occasions a simple way to cover a cake with royal icing is to give it an interesting textured finish. Swirls and peaks are both quick and easy to apply.

Swirls

Spread the top and sides of the cake with icing. With a palette knife, make swirling movements over the surface of the cake.

For added interest a layer of tinted icing can be swirled over a white base.

> **TIP** ◆ **ADDING COLOUR**
>
> For coloured swirls or piped decorations, tint a small quantity of royal icing by adding food colouring, a little at a time, on a cocktail stick. Use a spoon to stir the colouring into the icing until it is evenly blended.

Peaks

This finish is particularly popular for Christmas cakes because it gives a snow-capped look that lends itself to the seasonal decoration of Santa and sleighs. Cover the top and sides of the cake as smoothly as possible. Dip one side of a small, clean palette knife into some leftover icing, press down on to the icing on top of the cake and then pull it sharply away to form a peak. Re-dip the palette knife into the icing after about six peaks.

Piping royal icing

*By learning the basic techniques of piping
royal icing you can produce a wide range of iced decorations.
The designs can be piped directly on to the cake or
on to greaseproof paper and stored away, waiting for the occasion
that calls for something special.*

△ *A square cake can be iced with royal icing and then
decorated for a special occasion with straightforward
designs using one nozzle only. Beads in different
sizes, snails and squiggles are the only shapes used
but they combine to make this simple yellow
and white birthday cake.*

Fabric piping bag

Syringe

Paper piping bag

Plain tube nozzle

Piping designs

Piped decorations are made by forcing icing through a nozzle fitted into a paper or fabric bag or, sometimes, to a solid tube with a plunger. Being able to hold extra icing in reserve like this means that you can make fluid, continuous lines without a break and keep the rhythm going when piping the shapes.

Icing bags are available from good cake decorating suppliers, supermarkets and kitchen shops. They are made from washable fabric and are good for beginners.

Paper icing bags can be made from good-quality greaseproof or silicone paper. They can be bought ready made.

Piping nozzles are available in all shapes and sizes and some are designed to screw into a fitting on the bag. Start with a few simple ones and buy more as you need them.

Which nozzle?

There are many different nozzles you can use, but the majority of designs can be made by using either a tube or star nozzle. Take note, however, that the larger the nozzle, the stiffer the consistency of the icing should be. Beginners will probably find that using a fairly small nozzle fitted on to a paper piping bag will give them the most control.

The plain tube nozzle

This versatile nozzle has a simple round hole which allows you to 'write', make straight or curved lines, 'beads' or 'scribbles'.

Straight lines or curves are the simplest designs that can be piped. Practise pressing out an even thread of icing, avoiding thick beads at the end. If they do occur, neaten with a pin. Start with the nozzle pressed gently on to the surface. Then lift it up slightly and guide the thread of icing into position as it falls on to the surface. At the end of the line, press the nozzle gently down on to the surface to break the thread.

Beads are made by holding the nozzle just above the surface of the cake. Press out the icing, press down and pull up sharply. For a line of snails, press out slightly more icing, and move the nozzle to one side before pulling it up.

Trellis is made up from straight, parallel lines of piping. It looks particularly good edged with other piped shapes or patterns. Pipe straight parallel lines, leave to dry for about 20 minutes and then repeat the lines in the opposite direction to make diamonds or squares. You can add a third layer for a more elaborate built-up effect.

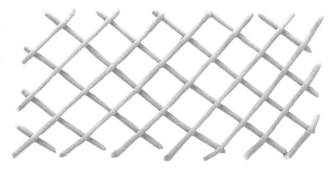

Scribbling consists of a squiggle pattern, comprising M and W shapes worked without stopping. The final effect is like random lace.

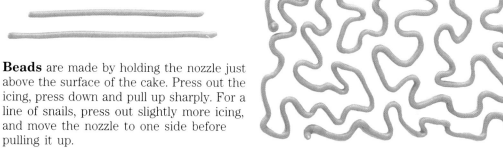

Writing in colour directly on to the cake does not allow for mistakes. Prick out the message on the cake with a pin first to ensure that it is in the correct position. Use icing to match the surface of the cake, and for contrast colours, paint with food colouring or over-pipe with coloured icing.

Preparing to ice

 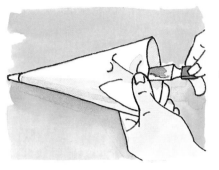 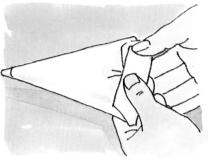

1 Snip the point off the paper bag and insert the nozzle so that it protrudes by about one third from the end.

2 Place the icing in the bag using a small palette knife. Push the icing down into the bag and press down on the opening to enclose the icing, withdrawing the knife from the bag as you do.

3 Fold the top corners of the bag over to enclose the icing until the bag bulges slightly, but not enough to push it out through the nozzle.

Icing a birthday cake

This simple cake is only decorated on the top – the sides are trimmed with a ribbon. To cover the cake with marzipan, see pages 8-9.

You will need
◇ Fruit cake 8in (20cm) square, covered with marzipan
◇ 2½lb (1.25kg) royal icing
◇ 10in (25cm) square cake board
◇ Side scraper
◇ Plain tube nozzle sizes 1 and 3
◇ Greaseproof paper icing bags
◇ Greaseproof paper and pin for the template
◇ Yellow food colouring
◇ Yellow ribbon for decoration

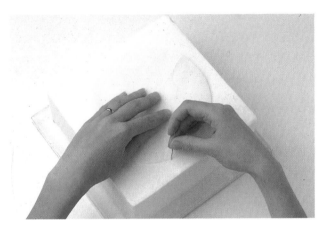

1 Ice the cake as described on pages 13-14 and when it is completely dry, apply a little icing to the cake board with the side scraper. Smooth the icing so that you have a flat surface on which you can continue the design.

2 Make a round template 6½in (16cm) in diameter for the central area on the cake by drawing around a plate or using a compass. Cut out the pattern from greaseproof paper. Hold it gently in position on the cake and prick around the shape with a pin.

3 With the white icing and no. 3 nozzle, ice the snails around the pricked line. Ice more snails around the perimeter of the cake on the top and where the cake meets the board. With no. 1 nozzle, draw random scribbles to fill in the outer area.

4 With the yellow icing and no. 3 nozzle, make three rings of beads inside the circle. Using white icing and no. 1 nozzle, add some outer petals. Ice four yellow beads within the central area. Tie a ribbon around the cake and pipe more flowers around base.

Making simple flowers

If you don't want to ice straight on to a cake at first, there are many decorations that can be prepared separately and then applied to the cake when they are dry. This avoids mistakes on the cake and is a good way of adding colour to a cake without risking smudging or affecting the pure pristine white of the royal icing.

Runouts are an example. The icing is piped on to a template, such as a letter or a number, and allowed to dry, then stored between sheets of greaseproof paper and placed directly on the cake when needed. This technique is described on pages 20-21.

Flowers with simple petals can be piped using a paper piping bag with the end snipped off into a V shape which leaves a slight contour on the petal. Do not add glycerine to the royal icing, and prepare batches of your chosen colours and separate paper bags for each colour. Pipe the flowers on to separate squares of greaseproof or parchment paper.

1 To make a simple flower shape, pipe one petal on to a paper square. Add another two petals on either side, slightly overlapping each one at the centre. The centre is made from a smaller petal.

2 To pipe a fuller flower shape, pipe five petals in a circle, leaving an area free in the centre. Into this space, pipe a further three petals, and then two more to make the centre.

3 To pipe a daisy shape, pipe five petals in a circle as in step 2. Using a plain tube nozzle, pipe yellow icing in a circle in the centre. Pipe a further two rings on top of this.

4 For a flatter flower shape, pipe six petals in a circle, leaving the centre free as before. Using a piping bag or a matchstick, drop a little white icing into the centre to finish off.

Royal icing runouts

*Decorating a cake is given an
extra dimension with the delicate shapes created by using
the runout technique. Special occasions can be
commemorated with letters or symbols to complement the
overall decorative design.*

Icing runouts

The key to making successful runout motifs is to have the correct consistency of icing. For the piped outlines the icing has to be light. When lifted with a spoon it should form a soft peak that bends slightly at the tip. The icing used to fill the shape must flow to the outline but still hold its shape.

Materials

Double-sided waxed paper for piping out the runouts. Buy a good quality paper. Don't use grease-proof paper as the motifs will stick to it.

Royal icing to make the runouts. Adjust the standard recipe for royal icing (see page 12). For the outlines add extra egg white. For the filling, water down the icing slightly and colour if desired. You will also need a **pencil, paper piping bags, food colours, no. 1 writing nozzle** and **tooth picks.**

1 Using a pencil, trace the motif on to the waxed paper. Position the tracing on a cutting board, with the tracing side down, and hold in place with a few beads of icing.

2 Fit the no. 1 nozzle to a paper piping bag and fill with the outline icing. Trace around the outline with a thin line of icing. Join the icing at the points of the wing. Trace in the small circles on the wing of the large butterfly motif.

△ Trace the floral circle and butterfly designs on to waxed paper and use as templates.

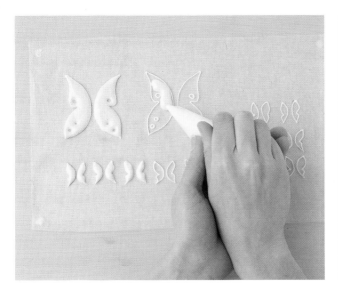

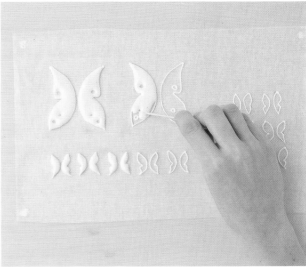

3 Pour some of the filling icing in to a second piping bag and snip off the end of the bag. Controlling the icing carefully, fill in the motifs. For the larger motifs, start from the edges and take the icing towards the centre.

4 Use a toothpick or pin to ease the icing into the corners and to smooth the surface.

5 Leave the runouts to dry overnight, until they set hard. Gently peel off the paper.

To decorate the cake

This cake would be ideal for a special occasion such as a christening party. The butterfly motifs sit with their wings up, giving the decoration a three dimensional feel. The top of the cake is iced to look like broderie anglaise by using the runout technique. Extra beads of icing are piped around the circles of the runout layer to add to the lacy texture.

The butterfly runouts can be made in advance, provided they are stored properly – keep them in a firm container, packed between layers of waxed paper. They are quite fragile, so handle them gently.

You will need

◇ An 8in (20cm) square cake, iced at least 24 hours in advance (see pages 13-14). Put the cake on a 10in (25cm) board and ice it to the edge.
◇ 1½lb (750g) of white royal icing
◇ ½lb (250g) of royal icing coloured apricot
◇ 2yd (180cm) of ⅛in (3mm) wide yellow ribbon
◇ A 10in (25cm) square cake board
◇ A no. 1 and a no. 4 nozzle
◇ Paper piping bags
◇ You will also need two cake decorating stamens, piping bags, tracing paper, pins, foil and pencil

1 Cut out the floral circle template and place on cake. Secure with pins. Then score lightly around the template with a pin. Remove the template.

2 Attach the no. 4 nozzle to a piping bag and fill bag with white icing. Pipe shells over the pin markings to make the template shape. Then pipe shells around the top outer edge and bottom of the cake.

3 Attach a no. 1 nozzle to the piping bag and pipe small circles randomly over the top of the cake, in the area between the template shape and the beaded edges. It is important at this stage to work as quickly as possible to prevent the icing from drying.

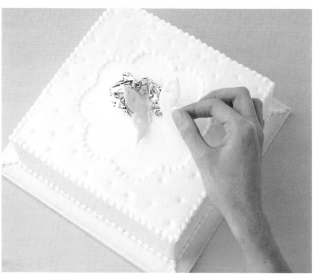

4 Take another paper piping bag, fill with white icing and snip the end off. Flood the area marked with small circles with icing. Work as quickly as possible to prevent the icing from drying. As for the runout motifs, use a toothpick to smooth the surface and push the icing into the corners.

5 To attach the butterfly to the cake, first pipe a ⅜in (1cm) length of white icing on to the centre of the cake. Place the base of each wing on the iced strip. Support the wings with crumpled foil until the iced base is completely dry. This should take a couple of hours. Repeat for the small motifs.

To complete the cake

1 When wings have set in place, pipe four shells between the wings for the body. Before the icing dries, push the stamens into place to make the antennae.

2 To make the broderie anglaise effect, use the fine piping nozzle to outline the holes. Add three petal shapes around the holes. Outline the holes on the butterfly wings.

3 Cut the ribbon in half and wrap a length around the top and then the base of the cake. Secure with a dob of icing. Add small butterflies to the corners.

Wired sugar flowers

*Simple sugar flowers, piped on to short lengths of
floristry wire, add height and softness to bouquets of moulded
roses. Use them as the finishing touch to a delicate
table decoration, as the decorative centrepiece for a special
cake or simply to enhance a pretty gift box.*

Make dainty floral sprays by piping
royal icing on to floristry wire.
Prepare the flowers well in advance
as they are made in two stages and
need to set both times for around
twelve hours. Before starting, cover
the work surface with greaseproof
paper and secure it in place with a
few dots of icing. The fragile look of
these flower sprays works well with
moulded sugarpaste flowers. These
can be made in advance, then combined with the wired sprays for a
small bouquet to trim a cake.

▽ *Pastel tones are an effective
choice for this pretty bouquet of
roses and dainty floral sprays.*

You will need
◇ Floristry wire
◇ Royal icing made with 2 egg whites (see page 12)
◇ Pink and blue food colouring
◇ Piping bag and no. 1 or 2 nozzles
◇ Greaseproof paper
◇ Moulded roses and leaves (see pages 47-50)
◇ Narrow blue or pink ribbon

Forget-me-nots

Dainty forget-me-nots are formed by piped dots that graduate in size.

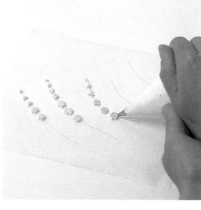

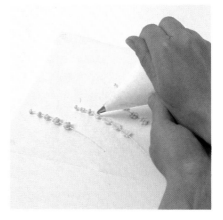

1 Secure greaseproof paper to work surface with icing. Cut wire 2-3in (5-7.5cm) long and bend slightly. Lay wire on greaseproof paper. Colour a little icing blue, and place in a piping bag fitted with a no. 1 or no. 2 nozzle.

2 Pipe a dot at one end of wire. Leave a small gap then pipe a cluster of 2-3 dots. Work along wire, leaving gaps, and increasing amount of dots until you have small forget-me-nots of 7 dots. Leave overnight to harden.

3 Peel paper away from flowers and turn flowers over. Place them flower side down on a fresh sheet of paper. Pipe more dots on to wire to cover backs of existing flowers. Leave for a further 24 hours to harden completely.

Lily of the valley

The white bell shapes of lily of the valley are made by piping along one side of the floristry wire.

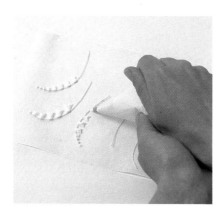

1 Place white icing in a bag fitted with a no. 2 nozzle. Pipe small petals along wire, starting with dot at one end and increasing amount of icing piped as you work along the wire to make bell-shaped petals.

2 Harden and complete other side of flowers as described for forget-me-nots.

Pink blossom

Small, white-centred flowers complete the display. The centre is piped first, then the petals. They increase down the wire.

1 Using white icing and a no. 1 or no. 2 nozzle, pipe a row of dots down wire. For some sprays graduate dots down wire.

2 Using pink icing and no. 2 nozzle, pipe small petals from each dot of white icing. Harden and complete backs as described for forget-me-nots.

To assemble bouquet

1 To assemble bouquet, press a small dome of moulding icing on to marble surface, foil or in position on top of an iced cake.

2 Secure the roses to dome with a small ball of icing. Press the wired flowers into the icing ball, filling the gaps between roses until bouquet is complete.

3 Cut the ribbon into short lengths and make it into loops by sticking the ends together with a small ball of icing. Press the loops of ribbon into the bouquet between the flowers.

TIP   STORAGE

◇ Once assembled, leave the bouquet for 1-2 days before disturbing. If it is used as a cake decoration, the bouquet can be assembled directly on to cake.

◇ Sugared flowers will store well for several weeks. Place them in an airtight container in a cool, dry place.

Basketwork

*Iced basketwork is remarkably easy to master
yet it always looks impressive — and if you find it difficult
to make royal icing really smooth, it ensures a
professional finish. The technique can be used to cover a
large cake or to make individual baskets.*

Basketwork is generally used to cover the sides of a large round or square cake, sometimes with an accompanying lid. The cake should first be flat iced (see pages 11-14), although the smoothness of the flat icing is not important as the basketwork hides any flaws. If you are using a lid, allow several days for it to set before attempting to move the cake.

The half-open lid makes an ideal place for either a simple arrangement of fresh flowers (a perfect solution for someone just learning to ice cakes) or moulded sugar flowers. The fresh flowers should be arranged at the last minute, while moulded sugar flowers can be made in advance and secured in place using any left-over icing. Marzipan fruits also make a good

display under the lid, particularly if the icing is a pale straw colour. For children, why not turn the cake into a mock toy box by filling it with 'toys' made from sugarpaste.

The same basketwork method can be used to pipe butter cream and chocolate. A chocolate basket cake, while impressive in itself, could also be used as a display case for individual chocolates.

Basketwork method

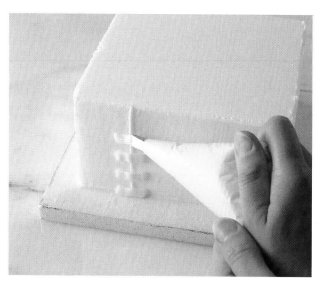

1 Pipe a vertical line of icing down the side of the cake using the writer nozzle. With basketwork nozzle, pipe 1in (2.5cm) bands across the line, leaving a nozzle-width space between each band.

2 Using writer nozzle, pipe another vertical line, just touching ends of basketwork bands.

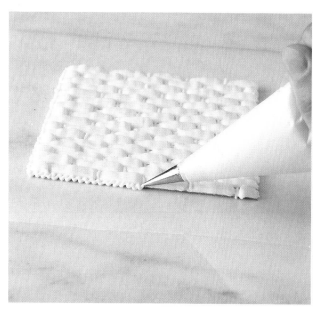

5 Cover the lid of the cake using the same technique, working over a piece of foil or baking paper. Pipe a wiggly line of icing around the edges using the writer nozzle. If you wish, pipe a decorative edge around the cake board in the same way. Leave overnight to harden.

Basketwork cake

A traditional square cake, covered with icing in a basketwork pattern is given another dimension when topped with a matching lid. The lid is iced at the back and supported open with wooden cocktail sticks.

Fill the gap between the lid and the cake with decorations, depending on the occasion for which the cake is made.

You will need

◇ 2 egg whites   ◇ Two icing bags
◇ llb (450g) confectioner's sugar, sifted
◇ No 2. writer & basketwork nozzles
◇ Cake 7-l0in (18-25cm) square, covered with flat icing (see pages 13-14)
◇ Thin cake card for lid, same size square as cake
◇ Wooden cocktail sticks

Mixing the icing

Place egg whites in a bowl and gradually whisk in the confectioner's sugar until the icing mixture is just peaking. Cover with cling film to prevent a crust forming.

Place a little icing in a piping bag fitted with a writer nozzle, and put more icing in a bag fitted with a basketwork nozzle. Do not overfill the bags.

3 Pipe more basketwork bands across the second line, filling in the gaps left by the first bands. Repeat the process around the sides of the cake.

4 As you approach the corner of the cake, space the vertical lines so that one line can be placed on the corner. Work with the corner of the cake facing you so that the basketwork bands can be comfortably worked around the corner. Continue as before.

To assemble cake

Carefully peel lid away from foil or paper. Pipe a band of icing along one top edge of cake. Press two cocktail sticks, ¹/₂in (1.2cm) into top of cake (each spaced equally from piped band) to support lid. Press another two sticks in side of cake just below piped band. These two will support the lid until the cake has hardened in place, and can then be removed. Fill the cake with fresh or moulded flowers, or other decoration of your choice.

▷ *For an alternative basketweave effect, use the basketwork nozzle for both vertical and horizontal lines. First pipe a vertical line, then overpipe this with the short horzontal lines. Run the second vertical line over the end of the short lines, and repeat as before.*

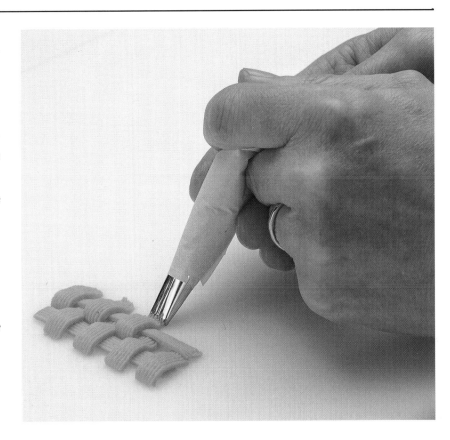

Individual basket

Small containers made from sheets of basketwoven icing are ideal for presenting sweets and chocolates. Use traditional white icing for formal occasions, or make brightly coloured boxes for children and fill them with small sweets such as sugared almonds.

You will need
◇ Icing nozzles and bags as before
◇ Small sweets
◇ Ribbon
◇ Rectangles of cake card each 2½ x 1½in (6.5 x 4cm)
◇ Waxed paper, ruler and pencil

▷ *Make an individual basket for someone as a special gift. Fill with Easter eggs, or choose a favourite type of confectionery.*

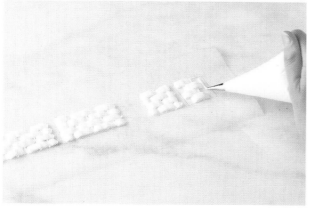

1 For each basket mark two 2½ x 1½in (6.5 x 4cm) rectangles and two 1½in (4cm) squares on to waxed paper. Pipe basketwork into rectangles and squares as before. Leave it to harden for at least 24 hours, then carefully peel away the paper.

2 Cover one side of each cake card with icing for a base for each box and leave to harden.

3 Pipe the icing with the writer nozzle along the edges of each panel and secure the panels together into a box. Pipe icing around outer edge of base and carefully position box to base. Leave to set for several hours.

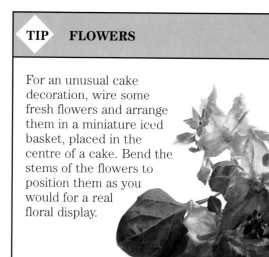

TIP FLOWERS

For an unusual cake decoration, wire some fresh flowers and arrange them in a miniature iced basket, placed in the centre of a cake. Bend the stems of the flowers to position them as you would for a real floral display.

Cake scrapers

*Cake scrapers with serrated edges can be used to
create a range of linear designs or swirls that will give a
sophisticated look to the plainest cake. Use them on
the sides or the top of a simple flat-iced cake and combine their
stripy pattern with a ribbon or floral arrangement.*

Decorative cake scrapers are a simple way to brighten up a plain iced cake for an informal celebration. The stripy two-tone effect is created by running the serrated edge of the scraper over two layers of different coloured royal icing, so that the bottom layer shows through. White icing is generally used for the top layer, with a pastel shade underneath, though this arrangement can be reversed for a bolder look.

Decorative scrapers are generally used around the side of the cake,

which can then be completed with a matching floral or ribbon display on top; with a little experimentation, the scrapers can also be used to great effect on the tops of cakes to produce a variety of symmetrical straight or curved designs.

Materials and equipment

A serrated cake decorating scraper, available from any cake decorating shop, is all that is needed for this technique. Alternatively, make your own from a card rectangle – cut one short edge with pinking shears. The straight edge of the scraper is used first to smooth the royal icing over the cake. The serrated edge is then passed over the iced layers for a lined finish that will reveal the second colour underneath.

Technique

You will need

◇ 8-10in (20-25cm) round cake, covered with marzipan and flat-iced with white royal icing (see pages 8-9 and 13-14)
◇ 2 egg whites
◇ 1lb (500g) confectioner's sugar, sifted
◇ Blue food colouring (or other pastel shade)
◇ Serrated cake scraper
◇ Palette knife
◇ Mixing bowls
◇ Ribbon or sugar flowers to decorate cake

1 Beat egg whites in bowl with confectioner's sugar to make a stiff, smooth icing which just holds its shape. Place half of the icing in a separate bowl and beat in a little blue food colouring (keep white icing tightly covered with cling film to prevent it hardening). Spread pale blue icing around sides of cake using palette knife. Use straight edge of scraper to smooth out icing, trimming off excess around top and base of cake (see page 14). Leave to harden for 24 hours.

2 Use palette knife to spread white icing in a thin layer over sides of cake to cover the hardened pale blue icing; smooth out icing with straight edge of scraper, as in step 1.

3 Draw serrated scraper around sides of cake, keeping hand steady and applying slight pressure so that fine lines of blue icing are uncovered. Work quickly, as the top layer of icing will soon begin to harden. Once scraped pattern is completed, trim excess icing off top and base of cake. Ice cake board and decorate cake with scattering of small sugar flowers and swirls of ribbon.

DECORATING IDEAS

Wave design

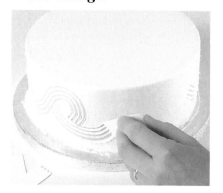

Make a narrow scraper from a slim rectangle of stiff card by trimming one end with pinking shears. Use it to create this wavy pattern by drawing a series of elongated 'S' shapes around the sides of the cake, extending the curves to about ¼in (6mm) from the top and base.

Semicircles

Use the narrow card scraper to draw a series of semicircular curves around the top of the cake, leaving a 1-2in (2.5-5cm) gap between each one. Make identical curves around the bottom edge of the cake, carefully positioning each one between the upper curves.

Parallel lines

This plastic cake scraper has a partially straight and partially serrated edge, which produces two parallel bands of white against a contrasting background of pastel blue (see picture on page 29 for finished effect). Use this scraper as described in step 3 above.

Marbled Icing

Moulding icing is a versatile, easy-to-use material for decorating cakes. For a special effect, try marbling the icing with food colouring to make a decorative embellishment to use on its own, or to make the base of a stunning novelty cake.

Moulding icing opens up a huge range of possibilities for decorating cakes — it can be rolled out with a rolling pin, moulded by hand or cut into any shape, rather like working with modelling dough. A few simple ingredients are beaten and then kneaded together to make a smooth, stiff paste before adding the colouring. Paste colours are easier to use than liquid colouring. For a marbled effect — useful for wood, water or stone finishes — colour is streaked through the icing by repeatedly folding and rolling it in. For solid colour, knead in the colouring thoroughly. For a patchy finish, for example for leaves, partly knead in different shades of the same colour.

Moulding icing recipe
You will need
◇ 1 rounded tbsp (7ml) liquid glucose
◇ 1 egg white
◇ 1lb (500g) sifted confectioner's sugar

Put the liquid glucose and egg white into a bowl. Gradually beat in sifted confectioner's sugar until the mixture is too stiff to beat.

Turn out on to a surface. Knead in the remaining confectioner's sugar to form a stiff, smooth paste. Wrap tightly in a plastic bag until required.

Crocodile cake
You will need
◇ 3lb (1.3kg) moulding icing
◇ Cornflour for dusting
◇ Assorted food paste colourings
◇ 9in (23cm) shallow fruit or sponge cake, covered with white almond paste and set on 12in (30cm) round silver cake board (see pages 8-9)
◇ 1 egg quantity royal icing (see page 12)

1 Start by making the marbled 'water'. Working on a surface dusted with cornflower, roll 2lb (900g) of the icing into a thick sausage shape. Use a cocktail stick to apply dark blue food colouring. Alternatively, tone down bright blue icing with a little black colouring.

2 Fold icing over and roll again into a thick sausage shape. Keep on rolling and folding the icing until it becomes streaked with colour. After about five rolls, dot icing with more colour and repeat rolling and folding another six to eight times, until only a little white icing is visible.

3 Dust surface generously with cornflour. Roll out icing so that it is about 1/4in (6mm) thick and about 3in (7.5cm) wider than diameter of cake. Place icing carefully over the cake.

△ *Appealing figures like this little bird are easy to shape from scraps of colourful moulding icing.*

4 Dust palms of hands with cornflour and then smooth icing over the top of the cake so that it falls down over the sides. Then ease it out carefully to fit neatly around the sides. Trim off any excess icing around base of the cake with a knife.

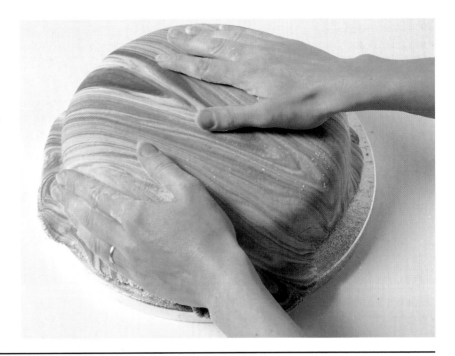

Decorating the cake

1 To shape crocodile, colour a little moulding icing deep green. Roll a small ball for the body, flatten slightly and place on cake. Roll a tapering tail and place on cake with the thick end about ½in (1.2cm) away from body. Curve thin end of tail. Shape head, tapering to a point for snout. Pinch icing at thick end to shape eyes. Using a sharp knife, make a cut for the mouth.

2 Put crocodile head on cake. To set the mouth in an open position, dust a folded piece of card with cornflour and use to prop mouth open. Leave card in position for 24 hours until icing has hardened. Meanwhile, use a knife to make criss-cross marks over body and tail. Add two blobs of white icing for eyes.

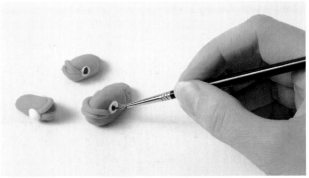

3 Shape bird's body, beak, wings, tail and crest using blue, yellow and orange moulding icing. To make up, brush with dampened paint brush and press parts gently together. Put bird on crocodile's back.

4 Shape small fish heads in red moulding icing. Cut small slits for mouths and trim with thinly rolled red icing. Use the tip of a knife to make fish scale markings. Add white eyes with centres painted blue.

5 To decorate edges of cake board, cover with thinly rolled green moulding icing. Trim off excess with a sharp knife.

6 To make the leaves, dot white moulding icing with green colouring, preferably in three different shades. To create mottled effect, knead colour in until patchy rather than even.

7 Roll out icing thinly and cut out leaf shapes in various sizes. Secure around cake. Make more leaves in brown moulding icing and secure around base of cake.

8 Place royal icing in a piping bag fitted with a fine writer nozzle. Pipe lines around crocodile and fish to represent ripples. Ease card out of mouth and make tongue with orange icing. Pipe small dots of icing for teeth.

△ *The patchy colour of these leaves gives them a realistic look.*

Draped icing

*Moulding icing, simply draped over the top of a
cake and left to fall in dainty folds around the sides, makes
an effortless and effective decoration. Embellish the
icing drapes with piping, or recreate the lacy look of broderie
anglaise by forming tiny punched holes.*

Loosely draped icing is the perfect way to decorate cakes when you want to create a delicate effect. The drape of icing itself can be trimmed in a variety of ways, from the clever broderie anglaise shown, to more elaborate, piped patterns. The simplicity of the drape could also be enhanced by adding a posy of fresh flowers to the top — an appealing idea for decorating an informal wedding cake.

Christening cake

The softness of draped icing, in an uncluttered broderie anglaise pattern, is particularly suitable for decorating a Christening cake. The broderie anglaise effect is formed by punching small holes into the drapes with a knitting needle and outlining them with piped white icing. Dots and other details piped in blue – or alternatively pink – add to the overall effect.

The draped baby's blanket, tiny booties and small mock sweets all help to evoke the mood of a Christening celebration.

You will need

◇ 3lb (1.3kg) moulding icing (see page 32)
◇ Cornflour for dusting
◇ 9in (23cm) round rich fruitcake, covered with almond paste and positioned on 12in (30cm) round prepared cake board (see pages 8-9)
◇ Medium sized knitting needle
◇ 8oz (200g) royal icing (see page 12)
◇ Piping bag fitted with fine (no. 1) writer's nozzle
◇ Blue or pink food colouring
◇ Fine ribbon

◇ TIP ICING

For best results always roll the icing into a circle 4in (10cm) larger than the diameter of the cake. Keep smoothing the edges of the circle as you roll to control excess cracking. Work fairly quickly so the icing will not harden before you can make the embroidery holes.

Forming the drapes

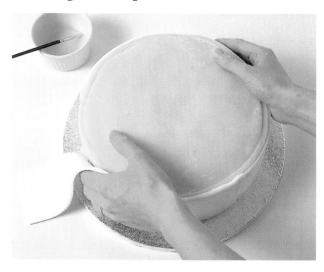

1 Lightly knead a little of the moulding icing on a surface dusted with cornflour. Roll into a strip the depth of the cake and long enough to wrap around half the sides. Press lightly into position. Roll another strip to cover the other half.

2 Dampen the section of the cake board that projects beyond the cake with a little water. Cover it with a thin strip of moulding icing, trimming off any excess hanging over the edges.

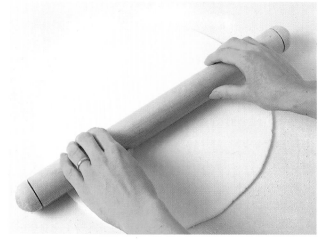

3 Reserve 8oz (200g) icing. Roll out remaining icing to a 13in (33cm) circle on a surface dusted with cornflour.

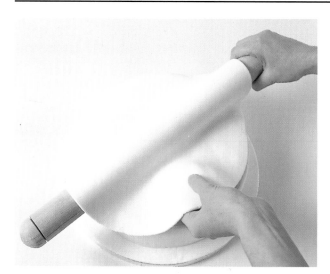

4 Lift icing up on a rolling pin and lay over the cake, letting excess fall evenly around sides of the cake. Dust palms of your hands with cornflour and lightly smooth the icing over the top of the cake.

5 Using palms and forefingers, accentuate the folds of icing around cake, creating more folds where the icing falls flat against sides.

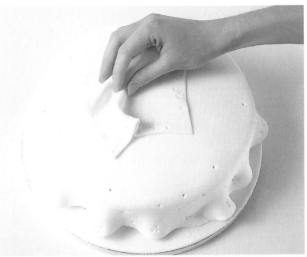

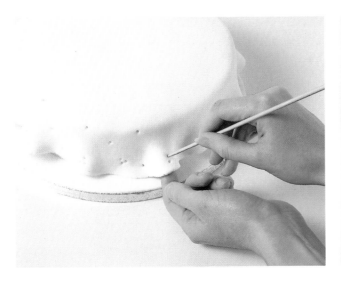

6 While icing is still soft, mark decorative holes in clusters of three and singly, using tip of knitting needle dipped in cornflour to prevent it sticking to the icing.

7 Roll a little more moulding icing as thinly as possible on a surface dusted with cornflour. Trim to a 5½in (14cm) square. Using knitting needle tip, make a border of holes around the edges as above, then carefully arrange the square on top of the cake. Allow it to fall in a couple of loose folds.

Making the booties

1 For booties shape two bases, each about the size of a grape, and flatten lightly. Mark holes in the bases with a needle.

2 For the tops of booties, roll out a little icing thinly and cut out two ¾ x 2¾in (2 x 7cm) rectangles. Mark holes in the rectangles with a needle. Secure rectangles over tops of bases.

Piping decoration

1 Allow the moulded icing to harden, then spoon a little royal icing into a piping bag. Pipe rings around each hole in the drape and baby's blanket.

Dolly mixtures

These little sweets are easily made out of trimmings from moulded icing. First colour a little moulded icing blue or pink to suit the rest of the cake. To make the squares, roll coloured and white icing into thin sheets, then press a white sheet between two coloured layers. Cut into small squares. To make the lozenges, make a narrow sausage of white icing with your fingers and cover with coloured icing. Cut into small cylinders.

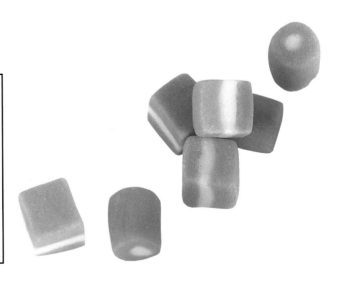

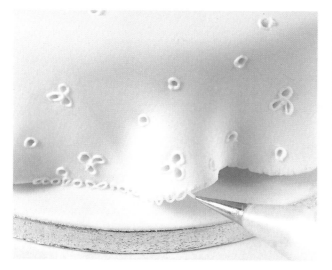

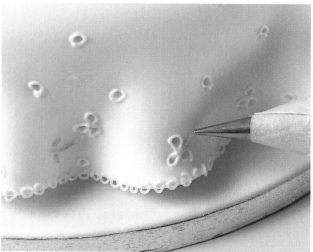

2 Use more white royal icing to pipe small loops around edges of drape and around blanket. Pipe the baby's initial at one corner of the blanket.

3 Colour a little royal icing blue or pink and spoon into piping bag. Use to pipe small stems, leaves and dots around the sides of cake and the blanket. Pipe a line of dots around the edge of the blanket and tops of the booties.

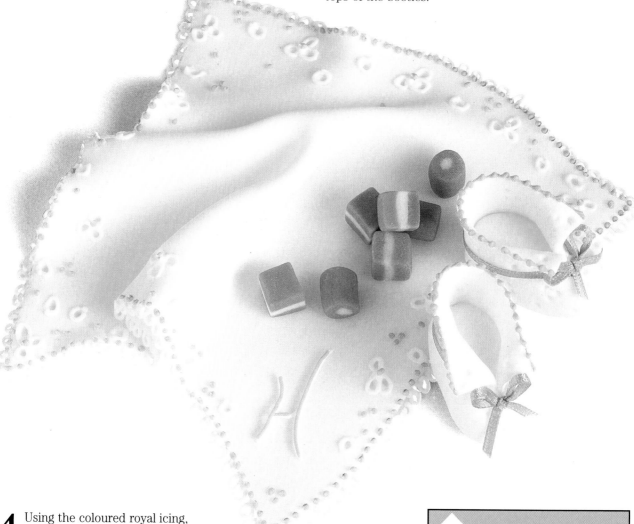

4 Using the coloured royal icing, pipe on top of the baby's initial to make it stand out.

5 Decorate booties with ribbon tied into bows and secure bows with dots of icing. Arrange little sweets (dolly mixtures) made from moulded icing on blanket.

TIP STORAGE

Make the cake two to three weeks in advance. Store, loosely covered, in a cool, dry place.

Garrett frills

*The classic Garrett frill can be used in a
variety of ways to add a touch of professional elegance to
the simplest of iced cakes. Scallop the dainty
frills around a tiered cake and add a pretty arrangement of
frosted flowers to create a stunning effect.*

The Garrett frill, named after its inventor Elaine Garrett, is one of the most elegant forms of cake decoration. Particularly popular for special occasion cakes, such as wedding and anniversary, these frills can be used to create a number of different effects.

For a pretty, traditional look, a single straight Garrett can be placed around the cake. More elaborate finishes can be achieved by scalloping the frill, as shown here, or by layering the Garretts, attaching first the lower then the upper layers. For an extravagant layered effect, two delicate shades of icing may be used.

Materials and equipment
Garrett frill cutters are available from specialist shops in metal or plastic. They often come with adjustable centre rings, which allow you to vary the depth of the frill.
Cocktail sticks are used to feather the edges of the frills once they have been cut.
Moulding icing, coloured as desired, is needed to make the frills.
A little cornflour dusted over your work surfaces and equipment will prevent the icing from sticking.

Method

1 Roll out thin layer of moulding icing on to surface dusted with cornflour. To prevent rest of icing from drying out, keep it wrapped in cling film. Dust Garrett frill cutter with cornflour and cut out ring. Discard centre and trimmings.

2 Cut through the icing ring and open it out slightly. Dust tip of a cocktail stick with cornflour and lay it on icing ring so tip rests half way across ring. Gently roll stick back and forth under fingers until edge of ring becomes frilled. Continue to work around ring in this way, dusting surface and cocktail stick with cornflour if they begin to stick. When the frill is completed, attach it to the cake as described.

TIP	FRILL CUTTERS

Garrett frill cutters are available from any cake decorating shop. However, as a more readily available alternative you can use a 3in (7.5cm) circular metal cutter (preferably fluted) with a 1½in (4cm) circular cutter to cut out the centre. If you use a frill cutter without a fixed centre, make sure that the hole in your ring is perfectly centred.

Tiered cake
Celebrate a special occasion with this elegantly decorated tiered cake. Here the Garrett frills have been placed in scallops around the cake, using a template to achieve a perfect symmetrical shape. The smaller cake rests on classic pillars which are supported by 'invisible' wooden dowelling – this allows layer after layer to be added if desired. Lightly frosted peach-coloured flowers to match the frills and delicately piped beads of icing complete the look.

You will need
◇ One 10in (25cm) diameter and one 6in (15cm) diameter round fruit or sponge cake, covered with almond paste (see pages 8-9) and white moulding icing (see pages 32-33) on 13in (33cm) and 8in (20cm) cake boards
◇ Greaseproof paper
◇ Pencil
◇ Scissors
◇ Knife
◇ 5in (12.5cm) saucer or bowl
◇ Needlework pins
◇ 2¼yds (2m) peach ribbon, ¼in (6mm) wide
◇ 1⅛yds (1m) peach ribbon, ¹⁄₁₆in (2mm) wide
◇ 1lb (500g) moulding icing
◇ Peach food colouring
◇ Equipment for frills (see above)
◇ 1 egg white
◇ Paint brush and a little water
◇ Piping bag fitted with fine writer nozzle
◇ 8oz (200g) confectioner's sugar, sifted
◇ 3 lengths wooden dowelling, diameter ⅛in (3mm)
◇ 3 cake pillars
◇ Frosted flowers (see page 42)
◇ Gypsophila or other spray flowers

1 Measure circumference of large cake. To make template, cut a length of greaseproof paper 2½in (6.5cm) wide and long enough to fit around the circumference of the cake. Fold paper lengthways to form eight equal sections. Make pencil marks on the fold lines 2in (5cm) from one of the edges. Using the saucer or bowl as a guide, join the marks with a pencilled curve. Cut carefully along the pencilled line with scissors.

4 At the tip of each scallop, cut vertically through frill to trim off excess. Repeat on next section of frill added and lightly rub frill ends together to remove join line. Repeat on remaining joins.

2 Using paint brush dipped in a little water, slightly dampen base of each cake and secure wider ribbon. Open out template and wrap it around large cake with flat edge around base. Secure ends with pins. Using a pin, carefully transfer template outline on to cake. Make and transfer template for smaller cake in same way.

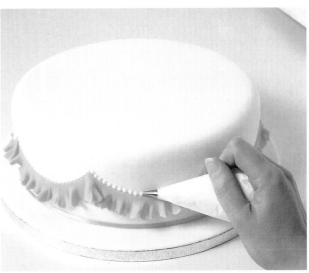

5 Beat egg white in bowl with enough confectioner's sugar to make icing which just holds its shape. Place in piping bag and pipe beading along top edge of frills. Finish with two small loops at tip of each scallop.

Stacking tiered cakes

1 Mark three pillar positions on large cake, each 3in (7.5cm) in from edge and an equal distance apart. Carefully press a dowelling stick, pointed end down, into cake at each marked point. Make sure the dowelling goes in completely vertically. Press each stick down as far as it will go.

3 Colour the moulding icing peach and make Garrett frill as shown opposite. To attach frill to cake, use paint brush to dampen icing just below template line. Then press frill into position so that its straight edge rests on the line.

2 Use a pen to mark a line on dowelling where it emerges from the cake. Carefully remove the dowelling sticks and cut or saw through the wood at marked line. Press the sticks firmly back into the cake ready to support the pillars.

3 With pillars in position over dowelling, carefully place top tier in position. Decorate top tier and centre of lower tier with frosted flowers (see below), securing each with a dot of piped icing. Finish with loops of ribbon and spray flowers.

To make frosted roses

Lightly frosted roses are an ideal way to decorate a prettily frilled cake, and with their sweet floral flavour they are fully edible.

You will need
◇ Several peach-coloured open roses
◇ 1 egg white
◇ Paint brush
◇ Small bowl of powdered sugar
◇ Needle and white thread

1 Carefully detach petals from roses. Lightly brush each petal with egg white, making sure they do not become too wet. Dust both sides of petals with powdered sugar and transfer to a wire rack to dry for at least two hours.

2 Once the petals are dry, take one and roll it up to form the centre of the rose. Wrap a second petal around the central one, and then a third to hold the flower together. If you are using petals of various sizes, place the smaller ones at the centre for a more authentic shape.

3 Attach petals securely by passing needle and thread through base of rose two or three times. Be careful not to pull too hard on the thread, otherwise you may tear the petals. Return frosted roses to wire rack as you make them and leave to dry for at least 24 hours. Store flowers in an airtight tin, between a few layers of tissue paper.

Moulded icing shapes

Delicate sugar roses, mouthwatering marzipan fruits, or even animals that look gentle enough to cuddle – all are part of the art of sugarcraft. Moulded shapes can be used to decorate cakes or as decorations in their own right.

Moulding shapes

Moulded shapes, in sugarpaste or marzipan, make effective decorations for cakes. However, marzipan can also be coloured, moulded and shaped to make imitation fruit (to decorate desserts, or even as after-dinner sweets). Flowers and animals are also popular motifs, which can be made from either sugarpaste or marzipan. The sugarpaste animals shown on page 46 could be used to decorate a child's party table, for example.

Both marzipan and sugarpaste are available ready-to-roll – all you have to do is add colour to create the shades you want, and knead the paste so that it is smooth and pliable. Use confectioner's sugar to prevent the paste from sticking to the surface. Some people prefer to use cornflour when working sugarpaste, as it has a finer texture.

Always mix plenty of coloured paste, as it is difficult to match the shade again exactly if you need more. Knead the colour thoroughly into the paste to ensure that it is evenly blended. Keep the paste wrapped while you work, so that it does not dry out.

Solid shapes

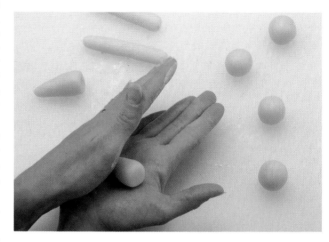

Make solid shapes by rolling the paste with your hands: roll on a surface to make a sausage, between your hands to make a ball, and between the base of your palms for a cone shape, as shown.

Blossom

1 Start by colouring the paste and rolling it into small cones. Push the broad end of the cone on to the point of a knitting needle to make a bell shape. Remove the paste and use scissors to snip down the sides to form five petals.

2 Open out the petals with your fingers, and mould the petals slightly, then add centres of white or coloured paste. The blossom can be arranged in groups, or threaded on to paper-covered wire if they are not intended for eating.

> **TIP   KEEP IT DRY**
>
> Sugarpaste and marzipan decorations can be kept for up to two months in an air-tight container.
>
> Leave the decorations to dry for a couple of hours, then store them in layers between clean sheets of white tissue paper.
>
> If the paste dries out so that you cannot stick it to the surface of a cake, use a little water on a pastry brush to moisten it.

Hellebores

1 To make delicate, cup-shaped flowers, colour and mould individual petals. Prepare a cup of foil by crumpling the foil and pressing an egg into it.

2 Press the petals into the foil cup, moistening the base of each petal to help it stick if necessary. Then add ready-made wire or plastic stamens.

3 Leave the sugarpaste to dry out for a few hours before lifting the flower out of the cup. Arrange the flowers in groups so that the petals support each other.

Flat shapes

To mould flat shapes, like flower petals or ears, take a small ball of paste, and squeeze it between your fingers to the required shape. Dust your fingers with icing sugar to prevent sticking.

Applying colour after shaping

Use a brush to apply liquid colour or paste thinned with water. For a natural effect where colours merge, apply the colour, then smudge it with your finger or thumb.

Marzipan fruit

These miniature fruit can be served as after-dinner treats, or used as decorations on a cake or dessert.

You will need
◇ Yellow or white marzipan
◇ Cloves
◇ Cocktail sticks
◇ Orange, red, green, yellow purple and brown food colouring

Oranges

Roll the marzipan into 1in (2.5cm) diameter balls, then stick a clove into one end. Prick all over with a cocktail stick to produce an orange peel effect, then paint with orange food colour.

Apples

Roll the marzipan into 1in (2.5cm) diameter balls and stick a whole clove in one end, to form a calyx.

Stick just the stalk of a clove in the other end to make the apple stalk. Paint on red and green food colouring, merging them for a natural effect.

Grapes

Colour white marzipan with yellow or purple colouring. Roll it into lots of tiny balls, about ⅛—¼in (3—6mm) in diameter. Roll a piece of paste into a cone and stick the individual grapes on to the cone, brushing with a little water to help them stick if necessary.

Bananas

Using yellow marzipan, make sausages about 1¼in (2cm) long. Curve them slightly, then flatten the sides. Stick a clove into one end, then paint on streaks of brown colour using a cocktail stick.

Making animals

These sugarpaste animals are more appealing as decorations than sweetmeats. Use a single animal to decorate a cake, or develop the idea to create a family of cats or a farmyard scene.

You will need
◇ Sugarpaste (see page 32)
◇ Yellow, red, pink, green and brown food colour
◇ Confectioner's sugar or cornflower
◇ Cocktail sticks
◇ Sieve
◇ Silver balls

Cat

Start with a white paste ball for the body, about 2in (5cm) in diameter. Roll a long sausage of paste and cut off two short front legs and a long tail. Mould the hind legs. Flatten the ends of the legs to form feet, and use a knife to mark toes. Make two small tapered triangles for the ears. Assemble these pieces and paint with orange food dye.

Make a white bib, three white patches for cheeks and chin, a pink nose and two green eyes. Add these features, finishing with silver balls for the eyes.

Pig

Roll out a fat, tapering sausage in pink sugarpaste, and squeeze the end to form a snout. Use a cocktail stick to make holes for the nostrils and a curved line for the mouth. Mould legs and a curly tail, and stick them to the body, moistening with water if necessary. Add white discs and silver balls for the eyes.

Sheep

Start with a white, slightly arched sausage for the body. In brown sugarpaste, make a flattened brown cone shape for the head; make a brown roll and cut four short legs. Assemble the pieces, then rub white sugarpaste through a sieve to make the woolly coat, and lay this on the body. Use yellow sugarpaste to form the horns, rolling it into two tapering sausages, then curling each round, and use a knife to make markings around the outer edge of the curve. Finally, add white discs and silver balls for the eyes.

Moulded sugar flowers

*A colourful floral arrangement is one of the
most stunning ways to decorate a simple iced cake — and you
need not restrict yourself to using real flowers.
Moulding icing can be used to shape any flower you like,
in any colour or combination of shades.*

Depending on their complexity, moulded sugar flowers are either made one petal at a time and then assembled, like orchids and lilies or as a single unit, like summer blossoms. Both techniques can be easily adapted to make any flower of your choice, real or imaginary. For extra colour and realism, paint the flowers with food colouring;

wire stamens add the final touch.

Moulded sugar flowers look most effective when arranged on top of a simple iced cake, as part of a carefully planned colour scheme. Use soft, pastel tones of yellow and cream, or stronger summer shades like those pictured here, or for a really adventurous, tropical look, use bright red, purple and orange icing to create exotic blooms. If possible, do not ice the cake until

the flowers have fully dried and hardened, when you can be sure of their exact colour and choose the shade of the cake icing accordingly.

To give the arrangement more height, some of the flowers are mounted on thin wire 'stems'; use stems for the smaller, lighter flowers only, like the blossoms. Complete the cake with a few scattered moulded rose petals and a wide satin ribbon.

Lilies

The lily's long, slim petals add a touch of classic elegance to a floral arrangement. Make the flowers in two or three co-ordinated pastel shades to add colour and variety to the display.

You will need
◇ Quantity of home-made or shop-bought moulding icing
◇ Small amount of royal icing (see page 12)
◇ Pink and cream or yellow food colouring
◇ Rolling pin
◇ Cornflour
◇ Small, fine-bladed knife
◇ Aluminium foil
◇ Fine paint brush
◇ Flower stamens (available from cake decorating shops)

1 Colour half the moulding icing pale pink and the other half cream or pale yellow. Roll the icing out on a surface lightly dusted with cornflour, to form a thin layer. Use fine-bladed knife to cut out slim, pointed leaf shapes for lily petals: make each shape about 2¼in (6cm) long and ¾in (2cm) wide across the centre. Cut out five petals of the same colour for each flower.

2 Make a small cone of aluminium foil by moulding it over your finger, and stand it upright on the work surface. Dust the foil cone generously with cornflour to prevent the finished flower sticking to it. Place a blob of moulding icing over the top of the cone, and brush it with a dampened paint brush to make the surface slightly sticky.

3 Position petals one by one around foil cone so that one end of each petal is secured to blob of icing at tip; use five petals per flower. Overlap the petals slightly as shown, dampening them where they overlap to secure firmly. Gently bend the tips of the petals outwards to form an open lily shape. Leave to harden for at least 24 hours.

4 When the lily is hard, carefully twist it away from the foil cone. Lay flower on its side and pipe dots of white or cream royal icing into its centre. Gently press a few artificial stamens into flower centre and leave to harden.

Orchids

Exotic orchids take slightly more time and patience to make than most moulded sugar flowers, but the results are strikingly realistic. Each of the orchid's petals is different and needs individual shaping before the flower is assembled and dotted with colour.

You will need
◇ Quantity of home-made or shop-bought moulding icing
◇ Orchid cutters (usually available in sets of three differently sized cutters from cake decorating shops)
◇ Cornflour
◇ Rolling pin
◇ Aluminium foil
◇ Empty cardboard egg box
◇ Fine paint brush
◇ Red and peach food colouring

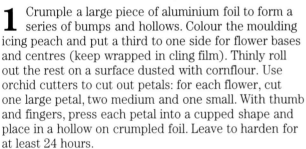

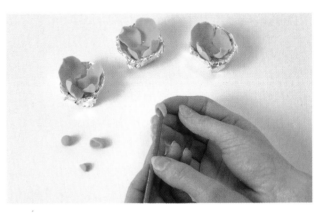

1 Crumple a large piece of aluminium foil to form a series of bumps and hollows. Colour the moulding icing peach and put a third to one side for flower bases and centres (keep wrapped in cling film). Thinly roll out the rest on a surface dusted with cornflour. Use orchid cutters to cut out petals: for each flower, cut one large petal, two medium and one small. With thumb and fingers, press each petal into a cupped shape and place in a hollow on crumpled foil. Leave to harden for at least 24 hours.

3 To make the tiny central petals of the orchid, roll a little of the remaining moulding icing into a small ball. Press tip of fine paint brush into centre of ball to make a cavity, and gently pull one side of ball, elongating it to form slipper-shaped orchid lip. Make another tiny petal by wrapping a small dot of moulding icing around the handle of the paint brush. Dampen the two central petals and carefully secure to centre of orchid. Leave the flower to harden for at least 24 hours.

2 To assemble the flowers, cut the cardboard egg box into individual egg containers and line with aluminium foil. Place a large blob of moulding icing in base of each container. Dampen blob with paint brush to make it slightly sticky, then carefully assemble petals in container, gently pressing ends of each petal into blob of icing to secure; begin with largest orchid petal, then place one medium-sized petal on either side. Place the smallest petal opposite the largest petal.

4 When flowers have fully hardened, use a fine paint brush to decorate orchid petals with small dots of red or dark peach food colouring. Leave to dry, then remove from foil moulds.

TIP	MAKING PETALS

Make only a few petals at a time. Moulding icing soon forms a crust, particularly in a warm room.

Blossoms

Delicate blossoms can be scattered around the edges of the arrangement, or mounted on wire stems to give the display more height. Their petals are made as a single unit, making the flowers fairly quick to assemble compared to the larger blooms.

You will need

◇ Quantity of home-made or shop-bought moulding icing
◇ Medium-sized blossom cutter (or use a five-point star cutter)
◇ Small calyx cutter (or use a small star cutter)
◇ Florists' wire
◇ Food colouring in pink, cream or yellow, green, brown

◇ Rolling pin
◇ Cornflour
◇ Cocktail stick
◇ Fine paint brush
◇ Flower stamens (available from cake decorating shops)
◇ Scissors to trim stamens

1 For stems, cut several 4in (10cm) lengths of florists' wire and bend each into a gentle curve. Colour a little icing green and thinly roll out on surface dusted with cornflour. Cut out calyx shapes with small cutter. Gently press one on to end of each wire stem.

4 Roll remaining yellow or cream icing into small dots and place one at centre of each blossom. Trim stamens to very short length and gently press a few into soft centre of each flower.

5 To finish, use pale brown food colouring and fine paint brush to add the delicate veins of the flower petals.

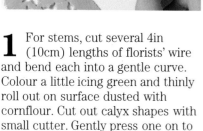

2 Colour bulk of remaining icing pink for petals, and the rest yellow or cream for flower centres. On cornfloured surface, roll out pink icing a little more thickly than for other flowers and cut out blossom shapes. Dip tip of cocktail stick in cornflour and roll around edges of flower shapes to give delicately fluted edge.

3 Dampen bases of petals and secure to calyces. Leave to harden for at least 24 hours.

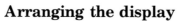

Rose petals

Fill any spaces in your moulded sugar flower arrangement with a few scattered rose petals. Make in the same way as the outer orchid petals (see step 1 of orchids) and leave to harden on crumpled foil. Use soft red or deep peach icing to add colour and depth to the pastel shades of the other flowers.

Arranging the display

Start by arranging the larger flowers on the cake, securing with a little icing. Use dots of moulding icing to prop up the flowers at attractive angles, particularly those with striking centres, like the orchids. Add flowers mounted on stems last: carefully press the wire into the cake, arranging the flowers at the most effective height and angle. Finally, secure petals in and around the display, and trailing over the edge of the cake to create a lightly scattered effect.

Brush embroidery

*For a really special cake decoration, brush
embroidery is well worth the time and effort it requires. By
carefully piping designs and adding texture with
delicate strokes of a fine paint brush, an interesting effect can
be created that closely resembles embroidery.*

Brush embroidery work can be used along with other decorations on a cake, such as moulded icing flowers or piped flowers, or on its own to build up a complete picture in icing. It can be worked directly on to the cake or on a plaque that is transferred on to the cake once it has been completed. Because of its textured finish, this technique is most suitable for shapes which have a distinctive, yet delicate natural texture such as flowers.

Although a little practice is required to perfect brush embroidery, it must be worked quickly so that the design is complete before the icing dries. For this reason only a small area should be worked at a time. Colour and definition can be added when the icing has dried.

To decorate a cake
You will need

◇ 10 x 8in (25.5 x 20.5cm) oval rich fruit or sponge cake, covered with almond paste (see pages 8-9) and soft green moulding icing (see pages 32-33) and set on a silver cake board
◇ 8oz (225g) white moulding icing
◇ Cornflour for dusting
◇ Green, pink, red and blue food colourings
◇ 2 egg whites
◇ Approximately 1lb (450g) confectioner's sugar, sifted
◇ Cake decorating stamens
◇ 1⅛yd (1m) dark green ribbon, about 2in (5cm) wide
◇ 2 greaseproof piping bags
◇ No. 2 writer's nozzle
◇ Fine paint brush
◇ Medium star nozzle for piping scallops around plaque

1 Trace the template on page 54 on to greaseproof paper and cut round the oval-shaped border. Reserve a small ball of the moulding icing. Colour the remainder very pale green. On a surface dusted with cornflour roll out the icing until it is slightly larger than the template. Lay the template over the icing and cut round it with a sharp knife to give an oval-shaped plaque. Ensure the edge is smooth.

2 Transfer plaque to foil or waxed paper and leave to harden for at least 24 hours. Lay template over plaque, traced side facing down, and pencil over traced line so that design is transferred to icing surface.

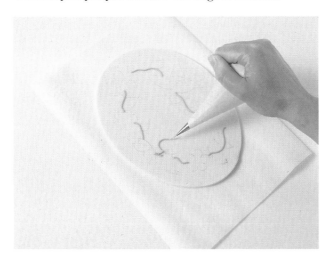

3 Place the egg whites in a bowl and gradually beat in the confectioner's sugar until mixture just holds its shape. (You may need a little less, or a little more confectioner's sugar than stated, depending on the size of the eggs used.) Colour half the remaining icing deeper green than that used on the plaque. Spoon into a piping bag fitted with a no. 2 writer nozzle. Pipe over stem lines and the outline of one side of one leaf.

4 Lightly dampen paint brush and brush through leaf icing towards centre to create leaf design. Repeat technique to form second half of leaf and then remaining leaves.

5 Colour a little more icing blue and place in a separate piping bag fitted with no. 2 nozzle. Use to pipe over outline of one butterfly. Brush the icing into the centre as described for the leaves. Repeat the technique on the second butterfly.

6 Use the nozzle and white icing to make the two brush-stroke blossoms. For the remaining blossoms, shape small petals from a little pink moulding icing and gently press into position, securing with a dampened paint brush.

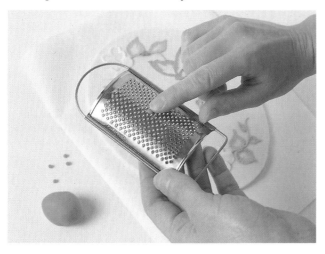

7 Colour and shape tiny red berries from moulding icing. You could roll them over a nutmeg grater to give them a knobbly texture. Secure them over design.

8 Using green icing, pipe a thin central vein through the centres of the leaves. Leave the plaque to harden for 24 hours.

To complete the cake

1 Add extra colour to the butterflies, using both green and blue food colouring — blend the two colours together if preferred, to give a deep turquoise colour. Use a paint brush to apply the colour so that it highlights the butterflies.

2 To finish the blossoms, pipe a little green icing into the centres. Cut the stamens close to the ends and press several of them into the freshly piped icing in the centre of each blossom. Use two stamens for the antennae of each butterfly.

54

TIP **FOOD COLOURING**

Most green food colourings are very bright. To give a more realistic shade, add a little black or brown colouring to dull the green.

3 Carefully lift the plaque from the foil or paper and position on top of the cake. Place more green icing in a piping bag fitted with a star nozzle and use to pipe scallops around the plaque. Pipe more scallops around the base of the cake. Tie ribbon around the cake to finish.

Trace diagram

Butter icing

*Quick and easy to make, butter icing can be used as
a delicious filling, frosting or covering for a wide range of
cakes. Use it plain or add your chosen colour
and flavour to taste. Butter icing works equally well spread
smoothly on to cakes or piped into shapes.*

Turning an everyday sponge cake into something spectacular, such as this delicious after-dinner gâteau, is much simpler than it seems if you work with butter icing. It is the easiest of icings to work with and can be flavoured and tinted to suit the occasion.

Butter icing recipe

To make enough icing to cover a 7-8in (17.5-20cm) square cake or an 8-9in (20-22.5cm) round cake.

You will need

◇ 4oz (125g) butter
◇ 8oz (250g) confectioner's sugar
◇ 2tsp (10ml) lemon juice
◇ Vanilla essence
◇ Wooden spoon
◇ Mixing bowl
◇ Sieve
◇ Choice of flavourings:
   cocoa or coffee mixed with
   water, liqueur or rind of orange,
   lemon or lime
◇ Food colouring (optional)

1 Place the butter in a bowl and beat with a wooden spoon until light and fluffy.

2 Pour some of the sugar into a sieve and sift on to the softened butter. Beat until smooth. Add more sugar. Repeat until all the sugar has been mixed in.

3 Add lemon juice and vanilla essence. Add additional flavourings at this stage if using.

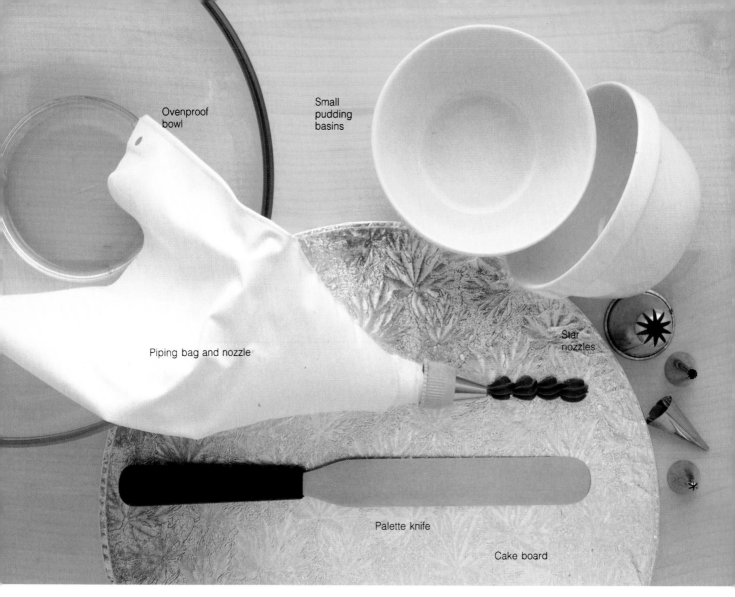

Ovenproof bowl

Small pudding basins

Piping bag and nozzle

Star nozzles

Palette knife

Cake board

Colouring butter icing

Bear in mind that if you are using coffee or cocoa as a flavouring you will end up with a brown coloured icing. For other colours use food colouring. Use sparingly, adding more drop by drop if a darker shade is required. For delicate pastel shades, see tip for American frosting given on the following page.

1 Add a few drops of food colouring at a time, using a cocktail stick.

2 Beat the food colouring or chocolate/cocoa mixed with a little water into the butter icing until it is evenly coloured and ready to use.

Simple decorations

Butter icing is soft and easy to spread and lends itself to a variety of finishes. Use either a palette knife or spatula to apply the icing over the entire cake, or use a piping bag and nozzles for a variety of shapes. For the best results use on the day it is made as butter icing hardens with refrigeration.

Flat icing

1 Spread butter icing to a thickness of about ¼in (6mm). Do not touch the cake's surface with your palette knife or crumbs will mix with the icing.

2 Use a palette knife and a light touch to smooth the surface. Dip the knife into a bowl of warm water between each sweep to keep it icing free.

Variations

◇ Use a palette knife and apply the icing in a backwards and forwards movement, creating a lined pattern. For the sides, start at the base and apply the icing with an up and down movement.

◇ Peaks and swirls can also be made in soft icing, just as they can in royal icing (see page 14), but make sure that the icing is not too firm, or you may find that the palette knife pulls some of the cake away with it.

◇ A plastic side scraper with a serrated edge makes an attractive finish if used to smooth the top and sides of the cakes. Use it to create straight lines or a zigzag pattern.

TIP	AMERICAN FROSTING

For a dazzlingly white icing replace the butter or margarine used in butter icing with the same amount of white vegetable fat and 3 tsp (15ml) of milk instead of lemon juice. This light textured icing is made in exactly the same way as butter icing and can be similarly flavoured and coloured. As it is pure white, American frosting is ideal as the base for pale pastel coloured icing.

Piping

Butter icing can be piped into a wide variety of designs, using plain, star, ribbon, basket base and frill nozzles (for how to use a plain nozzle, see page 16).

Using a star nozzle

Piping icing through a star nozzle produces a bevelled surface which can be easily transformed into stars whirls, scrolls and shells.

Stars are made by holding the piping bag or syringe in a vertical position. Apply a little light pressure to release the required amount of icing, then lift up sharply. Stars look very effective when piped close together, covering either the entire cake or just one area.

Shells Holding the piping bag at a slight angle, squeeze out a little icing. As you do this move the nozzle slightly forwards, then back again to a point just past the starting point, pulling off sharply. As the nozzle passes back over the central point squeeze out a little more icing.

Whirls, scrolls and coils are all made by moving the nozzle in a circular movement as the icing is pressed out. A simple circular movement, ending with pressing down on the surface and pulling away sharply will produce a whirl. Make the circle slightly less tight and add a tail of icing for a scroll. And if you move the nozzle along as you make the small circular movements, you will end up with an attractive coil.

58

Teddy Bear

One big smile deserves another and that's what you'll surely get when you present any child with this happy teddy cake. If you don't want to bake the cakes yourself, make up the face using shop bought sponge cakes. You will need one cake for the face and two smaller ones for the muzzle and the ears.

You will need:
◇ Basic sponge mixture
◇ 1lb (450g) butter icing
◇ Piping bag and star nozzles.
◇ 6pt (3.5L) ovenproof mixing bowl
◇ 2 x ½pt (300ml) pudding basins
◇ Greaseproof paper for lining
◇ Butter or margarine for greasing
◇ Yellow and blue food colouring
◇ Chocolate or cocoa
◇ Soft-centred mints, chocolate candy-coated sweets, coloured candies for features and bowtie
◇ Palette knife
◇ Cake board

1 Grease and base line the pudding basins and ovenproof bowl. Prepare sponge mixture and spoon a ½in (1.2cm) depth into each ½pt (300ml) pudding basin and the remainder into the ovenproof bowl. Bake the smaller cakes for 15 minutes and the larger cake for 35-40 minutes at 180°C (350°F; Gas 4)

2 Colour ¼ of the butter icing with chocolate or cocoa powder.

4 Set aside about 2 tbsp butter icing and colour the remainder with yellow food colouring. Flat ice teddy's face thinly. Keep dipping palette knife in water. Cover face and outer ears with yellow stars.

3 When cakes have cooled, divide one of the smaller ones in two and use for the teddy's ears. Place the large cake on the board, flat side down and position ears, securing with a little butter icing. Pipe a crescent of chocolate icing stars on each ear. Use the other small cake as teddy's muzzle and flat ice with chocolate icing.

5 Add a little more chocolate to the brown icing for a deeper colour and use with a fine nozzle to pipe the mouth. Position features.

6 Colour the remaining icing blue and use fairly large star nozzle to make the outline of the bowtie. Fill in with more piped icing and decorate with sweets.

Sugar dusted cakes

*These stunningly decorated cakes
will be much admired — and they are so easy to do. By
simply dusting confectioner's sugar over a stencil or
design motif you can transform an ordinary chocolate
cake into a work of art.*

Cake decorating can be a daunting task for the beginner. How many times have you wanted to make a decorated cake for a special occasion but lacked the time or the confidence to embark on an intricate iced design?

These cakes provide the solution. They are decorated by dusting the top of the cake with cocoa powder, then shaking confectioner's sugar over a stencil or motif placed on top of the cocoa-powdered surface. Whether you choose to embark on a simple design or a complicated one, the finished results will look wonderful and the method is very easy to follow.

Materials and equipment
You will probably have most of the materials and equipment necessary for making sugar dusted cakes in your kitchen already.

The cake can be ready made or one that you have baked, but it must have an even surface.

Confectioner's sugar, cocoa powder or **drinking chocolate** for decorating the surface of the cake.

A fine mesh sieve or **a new tea strainer** to dust the icing sugar over the cake.

Doilies or a **stencil.** Use a doily or make your own paper stencil.

Toothpicks or **pins** are useful for holding the stencil in place.

Stencils
A very effective design can be created by using a doily as a stencil – or you may like to try designing your own pattern. Draw or trace a design on to paper and cut out the motif you want to appear on the cake. You can also place 'found' objects such as leaves on to the cake surface and dust the icing sugar over them so that a silhouette of the object is left on the cake. Ready made templates for letters, stars and a wide variety of other motifs are available in kitchenware shops, or look for paper templates in stationery shops.

Design ideas
Simple designs can look just as effective as more complicated ones and you can be sure of success. Try dusting the top of the cake into bold geometric patterns such as a checkerboard design or even stripes. For more complicated designs use bought stencils.

For different design effects vary the colour theme – dust cocoa powder or drinking chocolate straight on to cake that has been coloured. Icing sugar, just crusted on to a pink or blue iced cake, will also look effective.

Method
Make sure the surface of the cake is completely even before you start. Cover the surface of the cake with a layer of cocoa powder or drinking chocolate. Lay your stencil or motif on to the cake and secure with pins or toothpicks if necessary. Gently shake an even layer of confectioner's sugar over the surface of the cake, using a fine mesh sieve and carefully lift off the stencil. The sugar pattern will smudge very easily, so store the cake in a safe place, well away from open windows.

▽ *Design your own stencil by drawing a pattern on to paper and cutting out the design. Practise on a work surface to see how the design will look.*

2
IDEAS FOR SPECIAL OCCASIONS

Wedding cake

*Combine all your cake decorating skills to
create a spectacular three-tiered wedding cake. Ice the cake in
soft ivory and surround each tier with layers of
delicate frills tipped with pink. With its elegant sugar flower
arrangements, this cake is every romantic's dream.*

For a traditional wedding cake, a rich fruit cake should be made several months in advance and drizzled with brandy before storing, tightly wrapped in foil, to mature. As a break from tradition, one or more tiers can be substituted with a lighter sponge or chocolate cake, if preferred. Whichever type of cake you choose, it must be covered with almond paste before icing.

This three-tiered wedding cake is covered with moulding icing and embellished with a beautiful pattern of ribbon inserts and Garrett frills. The decoration is finished off with exquisite flowers and delicate lace butterflies — all of them edible. The tiers of the cake are supported by cake pillars, wrapped in pink ribbon.

Make the cake as described here or, when you are more confident, adapt the techniques to make your own variations; for example, use slightly stronger colours or a different shaped cake. You could incorporate other piping techniques, such as scribbling (see page 16) or runouts (see pages 19-22).

Alternatives for the floral decorations could include wired sugar flowers (see pages 23-24) or frosted roses (see page 42).

The length of time required to ice and decorate the cake will depend largely on experience and practice, so leave plenty of time initially. Covering the cake with icing and making the ribbon insertion needs to be done in one long session before the icing hardens. Allow another session for making the Garrett frills. The flowers and finishing will take several hours but these can be worked in small stages.

Materials and equipment

Making a wedding cake requires a considerable effort, so it is worth investing in the right equipment. The following items are available from cake decorating specialist shops and some kitchenware shops.

Cutters You will need a plastic or metal Garrett frill cutter and small blossom cutters, preferably with a plunger attachment.

Greaseproof paper and **dressmakers' pins** are needed for marking templates.

You will also need several greaseproof piping bags, a fine writer nozzle, a fine paint brush and bakewell paper.

Covering the cakes

The cakes can be prepared up to 3 weeks before the wedding day. They are covered with marzipan, then left for 24 hours before icing. Remember to keep the moulding icing tightly wrapped in cling film while it is not in use.

You will need
◇ 3 round rich fruit cakes: one 12in (30cm), one 9in (23cm) and one 6in (15cm)
◇ 3 round silver cake boards: one 14in (35cm), one 11in (28cm) and one 8in (20cm)
◇ Apricot glaze
◇ 8lb (4kg) white marzipan
◇ 8lb (4kg) moulding icing
◇ Ivory food colouring
◇ Cornflour for dusting (see page 32)
◇ Pastry brush
◇ Rolling pin
◇ Sharp knife

1 Position cakes on appropriate cake boards. Brush largest cake with apricot glaze. Take 4lb (2kg) of marzipan, roll it out on a lightly cornfloured surface and use it to cover cake. Repeat for other two cakes, using 2½lb (1.25kg) of marzipan for medium-sized cake and 1½lb (750g) for smallest cake. Trim excess marzipan around base of cake with sharp knife. Leave for 24 hours. For more details on covering cakes, see pages 8-9.

2 Knead ivory food colouring into moulding icing and use to cover cakes (see pages 32-33); allow same quantities of icing per cake as for marzipan.

TIP ◇ ICING
Colour moulding icing in one go so each cake is covered with exactly the same colour.

Transferring templates

For perfectly even, symmetrical decoration around the sides of the cakes, paper templates are essential. They must be marked out immediately after icing the cakes.

You will need
◇ Greaseproof paper
◇ Scissors and pencil
◇ Saucer
◇ Pins

1 To make template for bottom tier, cut a length of greaseproof paper 4in (10cm) wide and long enough to fit around the cake's circumference. Fold paper in half widthways three times to give eight equal sections. Make pencil marks on the fold lines 3in (7.5cm) from one of the edges. Using a saucer as a guide, join the marks with a pencilled curved line. Cut along the pencilled line with scissors. Make sure all the curved lines are symmetrical.

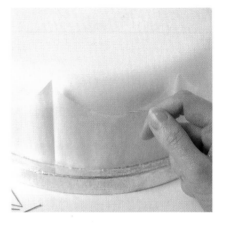

2 Loosely wrap template around cake with straight edge at cake base, and secure ends with pins. Using tip of a pin, mark outline of template on cake with pin-pricks spaced about ½in (1.2cm) apart. Remove template.

3 Make and transfer the templates for the other two cakes in the same way, marking the fold line on the middle tier template 2½in (6cm) from the edge, and the fold line on the top tier template 2¼in (5.5cm) from the edge.

Ribbon insertion

Ribbon insertion is a technique to create the effect of a single piece of ribbon threaded through the icing. The icing should have dried to form a thin crust on the outside, but it should not be set too hard.

The best type of ribbon to use is double-faced polyester satin, available from haberdashery counters of department stores. Use a different colour from the cake icing for an attractive effect.

You will need
◇ 2¼yd (2m) of ¼in (6mm) wide ivory ribbon
◇ Scissors
◇ Fine-bladed knife

1 Cut ribbon into ¹/₂in (1.2cm) lengths. Using tip of knife, make ¹/₄in (6mm) slit in icing at side of cake so that top of slit is in line with template outline. Press one end of a length of ribbon into slit using the tip of the knife.

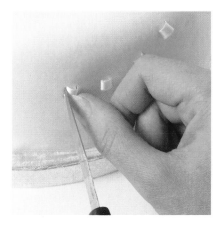

2 Make another slit ¹/₄in (6mm) away from the first. Press other end of ribbon into slit, using tip of knife to help ease ribbon into place. Continue ribbon insertion all around sides of cake, leaving a ¹/₂in (1.2cm) space between each insertion and angling slits to follow curve of template. Repeat on other two cakes.

Layered Garrett frills

These are a variation on Garrett frills. They are arranged in layers and given a dusting of powder.

A paper template is needed to position the layers. You can re-use the ribbon insertion templates by cutting them down — there is no need to make new ones.

For more details on making Garrett frills and attaching them to a cake, see pages 40-41.

You will need
◇ 2lb (1kg) ivory moulding icing (see page 32)
◇ Pale pink dusting powder
◇ 1 egg white

◇ 7oz (175g) confectioner's sugar, sifted
◇ Piping bag with fine writer nozzle
◇ Garrett frill cutter
◇ Cocktail stick
◇ Knife
◇ Fine paint brush

1 Cut off ³/₄in (2cm) from straight edge of each paper template. Reposition templates around cakes, keeping tips of each scallop in line with those of ribbon insertion, and use a pin to mark the line for Garrett frills, as previously shown.

2 Cover exposed edge of cake boards with thinly rolled icing. Beat together egg white and confectioner's sugar until mixture just holds its shape. Place in piping bag and use to pipe a small scroll around bottom edges of cakes.

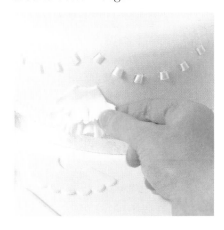

3 Cut out icing ring with Garrett frill cutter and frill outer edges with cocktail stick. Use paint brush to dampen icing on cake below tips of scallops. Cut a short length of frill and attach to base of dampened icing, so frilled bottom edge rests on iced board. Cut a slightly shorter length of frill and position it on cake above the first frill, so that the top of the frill comes almost to the line of the template.

4 Attach top layer of frill so that its straight edge rests on template line, with end of frill curving up into tip of scallop. At raised tips, and wherever two lengths of frill meet, cut vertically through frill to trim excess and gently rub ends together to remove join line. Attach frills all round cake and repeat, adding the layers of frills on the other two cakes.

5 Use a very fine paint brush to apply a light coating of pale pink dusting powder to the edges of the frills. Dampen the brush and lightly brush over the dusting powder to give it further definition. Allow colour to dry.

Lace extension work

You can give the cake an imitation lace frill made from royal icing. Delicate lacy shapes are piped on to baking paper. After hardening for 24 hours, they are peeled off and stuck on to the cake.

You will need
◇ Lace extension template
◇ Baking paper
◇ Pencil
◇ 1 egg white
◇ 7oz (175g) confectioner's sugar, sifted
◇ Piping bag with fine writer nozzle

LACE EXTENSION TEMPLATE

1 Beat together egg white and confectioner's sugar until mixture just holds its shape, and place in piping bag. Using lace extension template, trace about 100 shapes on to baking paper. To hold paper flat, secure it to the work surface with small blobs of icing piped underneath each of the corners.

2 Carefully pipe over traced shapes. If icing is a little stiff and difficult to pipe, turn it out into a bowl and beat in a few drops of water. Leave shapes to dry for at least 24 hours.

3 Gently peel baking paper away from the shapes. Remove them one at a time.

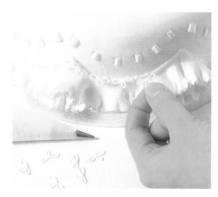

4 To attach lacy shapes to cake, pipe small blobs of icing, just

under ³⁄₈in (1cm) apart, along top edge of Garrett frill. Gently press lace shapes against blobs of icing, positioning them so they are almost touching one another and lie at an angle to the cake. Repeat on other two cakes.

Lace butterflies

You can use lace extension work to make all sorts of shapes. Forms which are naturally lacy, such as leaves, work well. These delicate and graceful butterflies are particularly effective.

BUTTERFLY
TEMPLATE

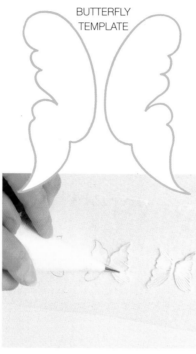

From template, trace five butterflies (three for cake and two spare) on to baking paper. Carefully pipe icing over traced outline of butterfly wings, then fill in the wings with finely piped lines of icing. Leave to dry for at least 24 hours.

Decorative piping

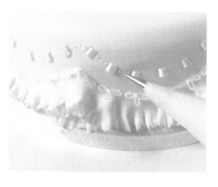

Use remaining icing in piping bag to pipe decorative dots between the ribbon insertion, following the scalloped lines on all cakes.

Moulded flowers

Flowers made from moulding icing complete the iced decorations on the cakes. Two types of flowers are used: carnations for the tops, and blossoms for the tops and also for the pillars.

A spray of carnations makes an elegant decoration for the top of a wedding cake. They are also one of the most successful types of flower to reproduce in sugar.

A scattering of tiny iced blossoms adds a touch of simplicity to the finished cakes. Real flowers can be combined with the moulded icing flowers for a fresh and natural effect but must be added last.

You will need
◇ Remaining ivory moulding icing
◇ Garrett frill cutter
◇ Cocktail stick
◇ Paint brush
◇ Crumpled aluminium foil
◇ Small blossom cutter
◇ Artificial stamens

To make carnations

Make a Garrett frill from ivory moulding icing, as described in step 3 of 'Layered Garrett frills'. Lightly brush unfrilled edge with a dampened paint brush to make it slightly sticky. Roll up frill to create flower and place in a hollow of crumpled foil to harden.

For a larger carnation, make a second Garrett frill, dampen edge and roll it around a small carnation. Make a total of about 32 carnations to complete the cake.

To make blossoms

Roll out remaining ivory moulding icing as thinly as possible. Use small blossom cutter to cut out about 60 flowers. Trim stamens and thread one through centre of each blossom. Leave to harden.

Finishing and assembling

To finish the cake, the tiers are stacked on cake pillars, then decorated with ribbons, icing flowers, butterflies and small sprigs of gypsophila.

You will need
◇ 8 plaster of Paris cake pillars
◇ 6⅝yd (6m) pale pink ribbon, ⅛in (3mm) wide
◇ 8 wooden dowelling sticks
◇ Small sprays of artificial pink and ivory gypsophila
◇ Royal icing in piping bag

1 Mark position of four pillars on bottom and middle cake tiers, making sure that each mark lies at an equal distance from the edge of the cake, and that all four marks are spaced an equal distance apart. Cut and position the dowelling sticks, ready to support the pillars (see pages 41-42 for information on how to do this).

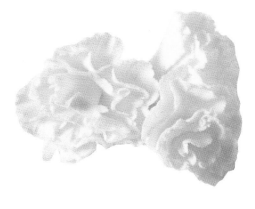

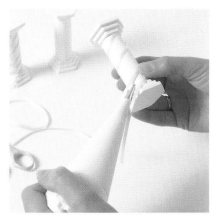

2 To decorate pillars, cut 24 lengths of pink ribbon, each one measuring 8in (20cm). Pipe a dot of icing at top of a pillar and secure end of a piece of ribbon. Wrap ribbon around pillar in a spiral and secure at base of pillar with another blob of icing, leaving end of ribbon trailing. Wrap two more lengths of ribbon around pillar in same way and repeat on each of the other seven pillars.

3 Pipe a blob of icing under each pillar and secure them to bottom and middle tier cakes, over dowelling. Use more icing to attach small blossoms to pillars and to secure carnations and remaining blossoms to cake around bases of the pillars.

4 Decorate top tier of cake with an arrangement of carnations and blossoms, secured with blobs of icing. Cut lengths of pink ribbon measuring 2½-3½in (6.5-9cm) and make ribbon loops by joining ends together with icing. Tuck loops between moulded flowers to enhance the display. Finish off with small sprigs of gypsophila. Complete arrangements on other tiers in same way.

5 Add butterflies to cake. Carefully peel baking paper away from butterfly wings. Pipe a fine line of icing near edge of bottom tier cake to represent butterfly's body. Carefully position pair of butterfly wings on piped line so that bases of wings are secured by icing. Place a small ball of foil on cake under each wing to hold wings at a realistic angle until butterfly body has fully hardened. Repeat on middle tier of cake. Add a third butterfly to top tier using same technique, but position it on a carnation.

6 Carefully stack the cakes on top of one another, ensuring that each new layer is centred on top of the pillars below.

Design library

▽ *The short pillars used to support this cake are hidden by the abundant use of fresh flowers.*

△ *Delicate extension work and dainty moulded flowers make this single cake look effective.*

△ *Special tiered cake stands, which hold the cakes without the need of pillars, are available.*

▽ *Cakes can be stacked on top of each other, provided the dowelling supports are still used.*

Gingerbread house

*A gingerbread house is the perfect
special-occasion cake for a winter birthday or festive
celebration. It looks most impressive, even
though it is surprisingly easy to make, and it will delight
guests both young and old alike.*

Rarely is something so enchanting so edible. This gingerbread house is set in a winter wonderland of creamy white chocolate, melt-in-the-mouth marshmallows, nougat, icicles of frosting, and drifts of sinful white sugar – and it is guaranteed to bring out the 'Hansel & Gretel' in all your friends.

You will need for base
◇ 6oz (175g) butter, softened
◇ 6oz (175g) soft dark brown sugar
◇ 3oz (75g) molasses
◇ 2 eggs
◇ 12oz (350g) plain flour
◇ ½tsp (2.5ml) baking powder
◇ 1tbsp (15ml) ground ginger
◇ 2tsp (10ml) ground mixed spice

To make gingerbread
Cream together butter and sugar. Add molasses, eggs, flour, baking powder and spices and mix to a soft dough. Chill for 30 minutes.

1 Roll out some of the dough on a floured surface and cut two 7 x 4½in (18 x 11cm) rectangles for roof. Cut two 6½ x 3½in (16.5 x 9cm) rectangles for sides. Cut out two windows on each side. Transfer pieces to a greased baking sheet.

2 Cut two shapes 3½in (9cm) on sides and base and 3in (7.5cm) on sloping roof edges. Transfer to greased baking sheet and bake all pieces at 190°C (300°F; Gas 5) for about 20 minutes, until they begin to darken around edges. Leave on baking sheet for 10 minutes, then transfer to wire rack to cool.

5 Use a palette knife to spread icing over the cake board, piling it up around the house to resemble swept snow.

6 Cut nougat into small pieces for steps and position at end of house. Colour a little ready-to-roll icing with pink food colouring, and use to shape small door. Dampen above steps and secure door in place. Roll thin strips of pink icing and secure inside windows for panes.

You will need for decoration
◇ 2 egg whites
◇ 1lb (450g) confectioner's sugar, sifted
◇ 1 1in (28cm) round cake board
◇ 2 ginger slab cakes
◇ 8oz (225g) packet ready-to-roll icing
◇ Pink food colouring

◇ Marshmallow logs
◇ White chocolate buttons
◇ 2 nougat sweets
◇ Pink and white marshmallows
◇ 2 small white chocolate bars
◇ Pink, green and brown chocolate candy-coated sweets
◇ Confectioner's sugar for dusting
◇ Greaseproof paper piping bag

To make icing
Place egg whites in a bowl. Gradually beat in confectioner's sugar until peaking. Cover surface with cling film to prevent a crust forming, until ready to use.

3 Spread a little icing on to cake board. Sandwich slab cakes with icing and place on board. Dot icing gently around side sections of house and press gently into position.

4 Dot icing around each end section and place in position. Dot more icing around edges of roof sections and remainder over sides. Hold in place for a minute or two until roof feels secure.

7 Cut marshmallows and press into icing for path. Cut white chocolate bars into rectangles. Dot back of rectangles with icing and secure either side of windows and door.

8 Cut a block of icing from ready-to-roll icing for chimney. Cut off one corner to give sloping edge and secure to roof with icing. Position piece of marshmallow log on top of chimney.

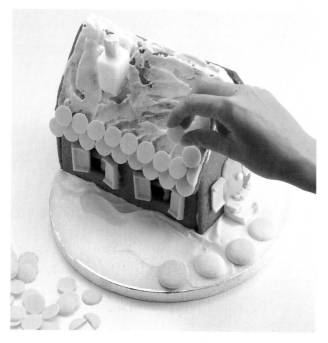

9 Thinly cover roof sections with icing and cover with chocolate buttons, starting at lower edge and working to top. Finish with a row of overlapping buttons along top of roof.

10 Place remaining icing in a greaseproof piping bag and snip off end (or fit with a large writing nozzle). Use to pipe 'icicles' under roof sections by piping a blob of icing then gently pulling bag away. Pipe snow on shutter sills and over door.

11 Pipe icing to base of cake at corners to resemble snow-covered shrubs. Cut chocolate candy-covered sweets into small pieces and press into icing.

12 Place a little confectioner's sugar in a sieve and dust over top of roof to finish. Keep gingerbread house in a cool, dry place for up to a week before eating.

Moulding icing figures

*Shaping moulding icing is rather like playing with
Plasticine — you can make it into virtually any shape you want,
like this colourful toy box filled with edible
toys. The icing can be rolled and re-rolled, shaped and re-shaped
until you achieve exactly the right form.*

Preparations for this charming toy box cake should begin well in advance, as the sides of the box need about 48 hours to set firmly. They are fitted around the basic cake, which can be plain sponge, chocolate or fruit, depending on personal preference.

When moulding the contents of the toy box, make plenty of 'bricks' – these are easy-to-make fillers and help to prop up the more detailed toys. The rag doll is assembled on the completed cake so that it can be propped up against the other toys and blocks.

You will need

◇ 31b (1.3kg) moulding icing (see page 32)
◇ Food paste colourings: green, red, yellow, blue, black and brown
◇ Cornflour for dusting work surface
◇ Greaseproof paper or foil
◇ Rectangular silver cake board 12 x 9in (30 x 23cm)
◇ Rectangular cake 8 x 4in (20 x 10cm)
◇ 2 egg whites   ◇ Cocktail sticks
◇ llb (500g) confectioner's   ◇ Small piece rice paper
sugar

1 Take four l0oz (250g) quantities of moulding icing. Using food paste colouring, colour one green, one red, one yellow and one blue. Leave the remainder white and cover with cling film.

2 Dust the work surface with cornflour, then thinly roll out half of the green icing. Cut out a rectangle measuring 8½ x 3in (21.5 x 7.5cm) and place carefully on a sheet of greaseproof paper or foil. Lightly score diagonal lines across the surface of the icing. Shape a rectangle the same size from yellow icing. Then shape two 4½ x 3in (11 x 7.5cm) rectangles from red and blue icing. Transfer to greaseproof paper or foil and score in the same way. Leave shapes to harden thoroughly for 48 hours.

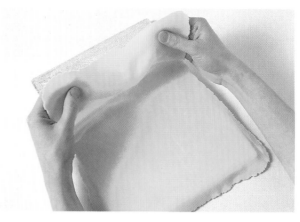

3 Roll out more yellow icing as thinly as possible until it is large enough to cover the cake board. Lightly dampen board, then lift rolled-out icing on to it. Dust palms of hands with cornflour and lightly smooth down icing. Trim off excess icing around edges of the board using a knife.

4 Beat the egg whites in a bowl, gradually adding confectioner's sugar until mixture holds its shape. Place cake on covered board and spread icing mixture over one long side of the cake. Put left-over mixture in a bowl, cover with cling film and reserve.

5 When rectangles are completely hard, carefully peel away paper. Position one long rectangle to iced side of cake. Spread icing on other long side and gently press next rectangle in position. Repeat with remaining rectangles making sure corners meet. Cover remaining icing with cling film and reserve.

6 Using palms of hands, roll a little red icing into a thin rope: cut into 3in (7.5cm) lengths. Use a paintbrush to dampen corners of cake with water and secure a length of icing to each corner.

8 For the books, roll a piece of white icing about ¼in (6mm) thick and cut into a square or oblong shape. Using knife blade, gently score three edges of the icing shape to make pages. Thinly roll out coloured icing slightly wider than pages and long enough to wrap round to make book cover. Dampen white icing and secure cover in position.

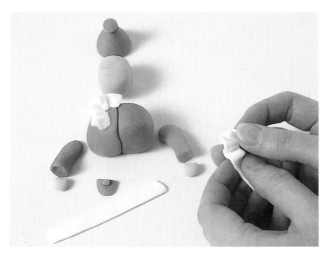

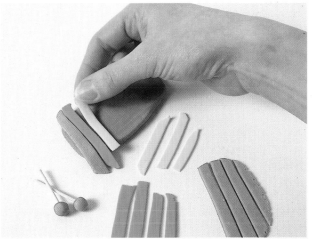

7 To shape the clown, roll a ball of red icing and another of blue, each measuring about ¾in (2cm) in diameter. Flatten one side of each. Dampen flattened sides and press together to form body. Roll a small sausage of icing for each arm and slice off ends. Press arms into position. Colour a little white icing pink or pale red and shape hands and head. Shape a blue cone for the hat and press a red bobble on tip. For the pocket, flatten a little blue icing and finish with a red 'button'. Thinly roll a little white icing and cut strips about ⅜in (1cm) wide. Pleat and press into position to form a ruff. Add eyes and a nose.

9 For the xylophone, roll out green icing and cut a rectangle measuring about 3 x 1½in (7.5 x 4cm). Roll and cut out strips of blue, red and yellow icing. Lay the strips carefully over the rectangle of green icing to make the keys and then trim into a tapering xylophone shape. Using the tip of a cocktail stick, pierce a small hole at each end of each xylophone key. To make the hammers, halve a cocktail stick and press balls of coloured icing on to ends.

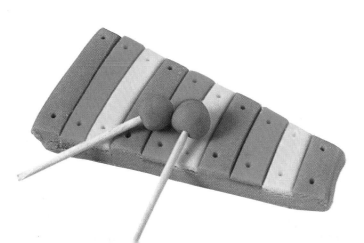

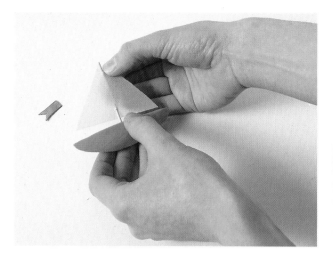

10 To make a toy boat, mould a little coloured icing into a wedge-shaped hull. Cut a small triangle of rice paper for the sail. Thread a cocktail stick through sail to make a mast and press tip into the top of the hull. Add a small icing flag.

11 Using remaining moulding icing, shape several more toys as desired, such as skittles, skipping rope handles, train, car, trumpet, beach balls, dolls house and drum. Shape a selection of small and large bricks to use as box fillers.

12 Cover cake top with reserved icing mixture and scatter a few bricks over. To shape rag doll, first mould head, hands and feet in pink icing. Mould the body, arms and legs in white icing to look like the doll is wearing a flounced top and pantaloons. Prop the doll's white body against a brick in toy box Secure head on to body and an arm dangling over box side. Add two blobs of icing for eyes. Using a very fine paintbrush, paint on features with food paste colouring. Use black for the eyes and red for the mouth.

13 Colour the rest of icing mixture yellow and place in piping bag fitted with a fine writer nozzle. Press a cocktail stick into back of doll's head to give support for hair. Pipe lines of yellow icing from head to top of cocktail stick. Pipe lines for fringe, then pipe more lines down the stick and on other side of head. Pipe curly hair on clown and add blobs of icing around drum.

14 For skipping rope, colour a small piece of icing with brown food colouring. Roll and fold icing until streaked with colour. Roll into a very thin strip and drape carefully over side of box in a loop. Arrange another length over side of box and secure to skipping rope handle. Secure second skipping rope handle to end of rope inside box.

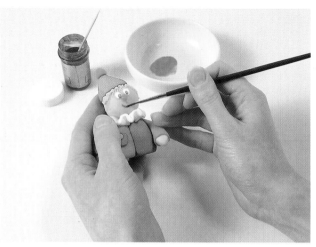

15 Using fine paintbrush and food paste colouring, paint features on clown's face. Paint features on remaining toys, such as markings on beach ball and drum, and windows on house and train. Add lettering to books. To finish, fill box with toys, propping up rag doll's legs and feet over other toys. Arrange any remaining toys around base of box.

◁ Skittles are easy to mould from coloured icing.

TIP   MOULDING ICING

◇ Store icing for later use in polythene bags or wrap tightly in cling film.
◇ Before cutting the cake, remove complete toys from box. If it's a birthday centrepiece, each child could take a toy home.

Treasure island cake

*This 'tropical island' cake, complete with a
chest of treasure, palm trees and a shipwreck, will appeal to all
children. The island is quick to assemble from slabs
of cake and it is iced in buttercream, which gives a convincing
textured surface to the landscape.*

Choose your child's favourite cake for the base of the island — a chocolate, orange or vanilla flavoured sponge, or even a fruit cake, would be suitable. The cake is assembled on a large cake board and can be iced a few days in advance, provided it is stored in a refrigerator or a cool, dry place. If you do not have a large cake board, usé a tray or chopping board and cover it with a piece of kitchen foil.

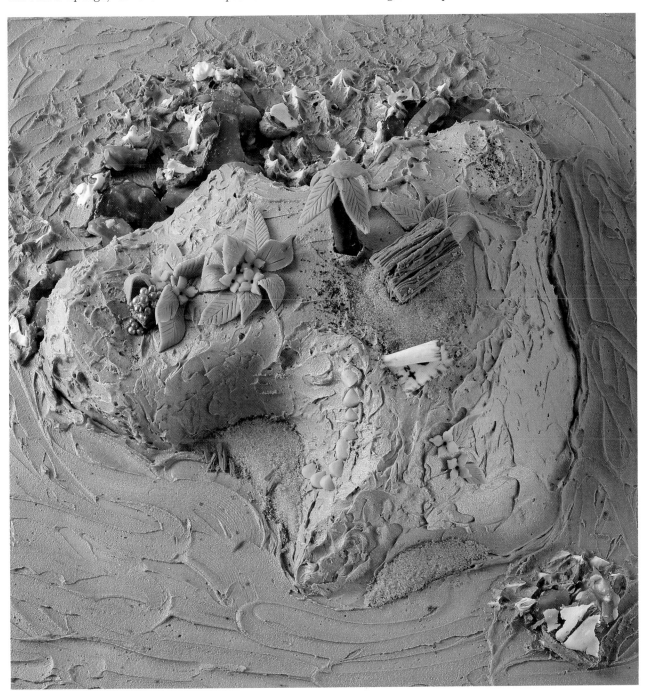

You will need

◇ 8-9in (20-23cm) round cake, about 1½in (4cm) deep
◇ 14in (35cm) square cake board
◇ 8oz (225g) butter or margarine, softened
◇ llb (450g) confectioner's sugar
◇ Green, blue, brown, black and orange food colourings
◇ 1 small chocolate-covered caramel bar
◇ 1 small packet ready-to-roll icing
◇ Cornflour for dusting
◇ 8oz (225g) bag of roughly broken peanut brittle.
◇ 3tbsp brown sugar
◇ Several blanched almonds
◇ 1 chocolate flake bar
◇ Coloured dragées
◇ Piping bag fitted with a large writer nozzle
◇ Egg cup
◇ Kitchen foil
◇ 2-2½in (5-6cm) round metal biscuit cutter
◇ Drinking chocolate
◇ Small flower or star cutter

Assembling the cake

1 Using a biscuit cutter, cut a semi-circle from one side of the cake. Using a small dish or saucer as a guide, cut a larger semi-circle in a position further around the edge of the cake. Trim one edge of each of the cut-off semi-circles, so they sit snugly against the cake.

2 Using a knife, round off some of the edges of the cake. Leave some edges untrimmed to represent steep cliffs. Assemble the island on the cake board.

Icing the cake

1 Place the butter or margarine in a large bowl and beat it lightly. Add the confectioner's sugar and ltbsp boiling water to the butter and beat well until the mixture is smooth and creamy. Reserve 2tbsp of the buttercream. Transfer a third of the remaining buttercream to a bowl and colour it blue. Colour the remaining buttercream green. Spread the green buttercream over the cake and smooth it down roughly.

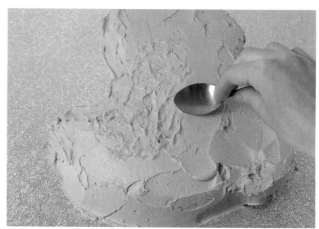

2 Using a knife or spoon, lightly fluff up the buttercream for added texture.

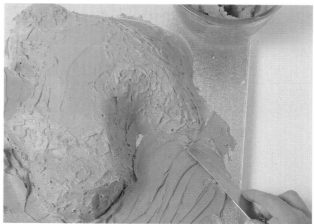

3 Spread the blue buttercream out thinly to cover the cake board, reserving a little for the rougher sea. Swirl buttercream lightly.

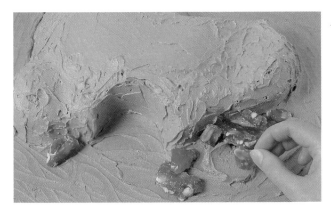

4 Gently press peanut brittle around one side of the cake (where 'cliffs' are steepest), pressing some right into the cake and others further out to 'sea'.

6 Spoon more blue icing around the 'rocks'. Using the back of a teaspoon pull up the icing to create 'waves' around the rocks.

5 To make the waterfall, place a little blue icing in a piping bag fitted with a large writer nozzle. Pipe a curving line of buttercream from the top of the island down to the sea. Add a second curved line, then pipe some more lines over the waterfall to build it up slightly.

7 Dot the rough icing with the plain white buttercream and, again, pull it up with the back of a teaspoon to accentuate the waves.

Trimming the cake

1 Take a little of the ready-to-roll icing and colour it green for foliage. Stiffen icing by kneading it in a little confectioner's sugar, then roll it out on a surface dusted with cornflour. Using the tip of a knife cut out 4 palm tree leaves, about 1½in (4cm) at widest point. Mark veins with the knife.

2 Line an egg cup with foil. Arrange leaves in egg cup with ends overlapping in base. If the ends of the leaves are too dry to stick, brush them lightly with water, then press them together. Cut a tree about 2in (5cm) long, from chocolate caramel bar. Press chocolate bar lightly into overlapping ends of leaves and leave for several hours, or overnight, to harden.

3 Sprinkle a little brown sugar into the 'coves' around the base of the cake. Press it down lightly. Cut the blanched almonds into small pieces and press them into the cake to look like steps leading up from the cove. Sift a small amount of dark drinking chocolate over top of the cake – to add to the texture of the landscape.

4 To shape the hut, cut 2 pieces of flake bar, about ¹/₂in (1cm) long. Press them on top of the cake. Cut another piece of flake, about 1¹/₄in (2cm) long and cut two flat sections from this piece for the roof. Secure roof in place with a little buttercream. Sprinkle a little sugar near the hut.

5 Arrange more leaves over cake. Cut another piece of flake and tuck it under leaves for the treasure chest. Spread with buttercream and dot with dragées.

6 Colour a little more ready-to-roll icing orange and roll it out thinly. Use a small flower or star cutter to make the flowers. Secure flowers to cake.

7 Shape a small rectangle of white icing for the map. Half roll the map, then paint edges brown and add simple map details in black. Place beside hut.

8 Carefully lift the palm tree from the egg cup and press it into the cake. Shape a small boat from the remaining flake. Lean it against a rock and complete it with tattered 'sails' made from icing.

▽ *The 'sea' around the rocks looks convincing — with the added advantage that both are edible.*

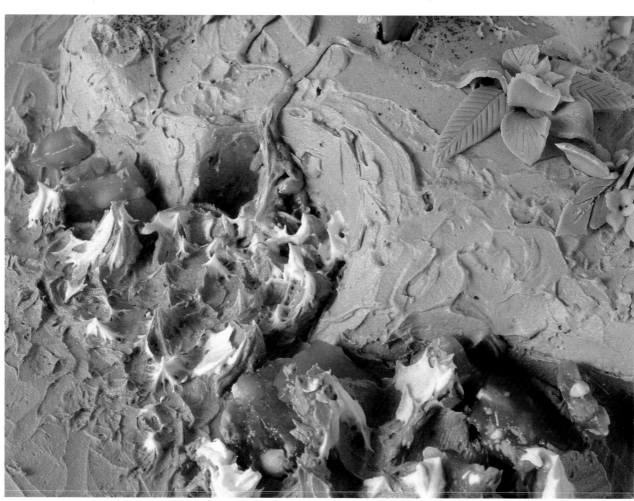

Yule logs

*A Yule log is as essential at Christmas as
rich fruit cake, mince pies and Christmas pudding — and with a
little creativity it can make a stunning table
centre-piece. Take a break from tradition and experiment with
unusual recipes and extravagant decorations.*

Yule logs are always a welcome addition to the Christmas table, particularly for those who have eaten their fill of rich fruit cake and Christmas pudding. There are potentially many different ways of cooking and presenting a yule log — it can be made from a simple, light sponge, or a crunchy, nutty chocolate mix. Whichever recipe you select, make sure you show off the log in its full glory — with imagination any basic cake recipe can be transformed.

The recipes can be made several days in advance and kept fresh in the fridge until needed. Alternatively, plan well ahead and store the logs in the freezer, on cake boards, loosely covered with foil.

▽ *Present a white chocolate log, as
the dramatic finale to a meal,
bedecked with shimmering baubles.*

White buttercream log

This snowy white Christmas log is made from a sponge base, spread with smooth orange buttercream and finished with a lavish dusting of confectioner's sugar. Echo the appealing 'winter' white feeling in the decoration by serving the log surrounded by white, silver or pearlized baubles and leaves, and a shimmering bed of translucent cellophane strips. For impact, dim the lights and decorate the log with glowing candles: slim candles pressed into the cake, or small night-lights. But remember, if you do use candles, keep them well away from other decorations and never leave the display unattended when lit.

To make sponge base

A Swiss roll sponge should be very light, but firm and springy enough to roll easily without breaking. Whisking the mixture over a pan of hot water ensures perfect results.

You will need
◇ 4oz (100g) powdered sugar
◇ 4 eggs
◇ 1tsp vanilla essence
◇ 4oz (100g) plain flour, sifted
◇ Greaseproof paper
◇ A little margarine or butter for greasing
◇ 13 x 9in (33 x 23cm) Swiss roll baking tin
◇ Saucepan of hot water
◇ Mixing bowls
◇ Tablespoon

1 Grease a piece of greaseproof paper and use it to line the Swiss roll tin. Place sugar, eggs and vanilla essence in a large mixing bowl and rest over the pan of hot water. Whisk for 5-10 minutes until mixture holds its shape. Remove the bowl from the heat and continue to beat until the whisk leaves a trail when it is lifted out of the mixture.

2 Fold in sifted flour with spoon. Pour into tin, making sure surface of mixture is level and spread into corners. Bake in preheated oven at 220°C (425°F; Gas 7) for 8-10 minutes until just firm to touch.

3 Dust another piece of greaseproof paper with sugar and invert sponge on to it. Peel off greaseproof paper used for baking sponge. Roll up sponge in sugared greaseproof paper and leave to cool.

To make buttercream

The rich buttercream used to fill and coat the Swiss roll has a deliciously tangy orange flavour. To further enhance the taste, try adding a few drops of an orange flavoured liqueur, such as Triple Sec, Cointreau or Grand Marnier.

You will need
◇ 6oz (175g) granulated sugar
◇ 4 egg yolks
◇ 12oz (350g) soft unsalted butter
◇ Finely grated zest of one orange
◇ Few drops orange-flavoured liqueur (optional)
◇ Heavy based saucepan
◇ Sugar thermometer (optional)
◇ Mixing bowls
◇ Knife for spreading

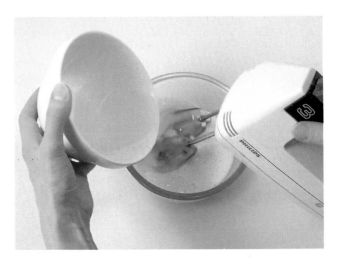

1 Dissolve the sugar in five tablespoons of water in the saucepan. Bring to the boil and continue to boil until the sugar reaches a temperature of 108°C (220°F) on the sugar thermometer. Remove from the heat. Leave for five minutes. If you do not have a sugar thermometer, boil the sugar until it turns a rich, brown caramel colour.

2 Beat the egg yolks in a bowl. Gradually whisk in the syrup. Place the butter in a separate bowl and whisk. Add the egg mixture, whisking well. Flavour with orange zest and, if desired, beat in a few drops of orange-flavoured liqueur.

3 Carefully unroll cake. Take one-third of the buttercream and use the knife to spread it over top of sponge. Re-roll the cake.

To decorate the yule log

The sponge 'log' is decorated with piped lines of buttercream and lavishly sprinkled with confectioner's sugar to resemble the snow-coated bark of a tree. Finish with sparkling Christmas decorations for a festive look.

You will need
◇ Remainder of buttercream
◇ Confectioner's sugar for dusting
◇ A thin cake board about 14 x 9in (35 x 23cm)
◇ Knife for spreading
◇ Piping bag fitted with star nozzle
◇ Small sieve
◇ Wired white or silver leaves (available from cake decorating shops)
◇ Christmas decorations, such as clear or pearlized baubles and translucent shredded film strips (available from department stores, gift shops and some stationers)

1 Spread cake board very lightly with buttercream. Sprinkle board with confectioner's sugar and place log in centre – the buttercream will help hold both the sugar coating and the log in place. Use knife to thinly spread a little buttercream over ends and then sides of log. Smooth the cream with a knife.

2 Place remaining buttercream in piping bag fitted with star nozzle and pipe lines along whole length of log, over top and sides.

3 Dust log lavishly with confectioner's sugar and sprinkle more over the board in any areas that remain uncovered.

4 Carefully decorate log with leaves and selection of Christmas baubles. Place in a bed of shredded translucent film strips or surround with candles, as shown in main picture.

Chocolate coin log

This rich truffle log is moulded from a chocolate, nut and crunchy cookie mixture and coated with smooth layers of white and dark chocolate. Decorate the log with chocolate flakes, gold marzipan strips and a shower of gold chocolate coins.

To make log

The chocolate log is not baked – simply place the moulded mixture in the fridge to harden for a few hours before decorating.

You will need

◇ 8oz (200g) plain chocolate, broken into pieces
◇ 2tbsp brandy or rum
◇ 8oz (200g) soft unsalted butter
◇ 1oz (25g) confectioner's sugar
◇ 2 egg yolks
◇ 4oz (100g) ground almonds
◇ 1oz (25g) cocoa powder
◇ 4oz (100g) shortbread or plain sweet cookies, roughly broken
◇ 2oz (50g) walnuts, roughly broken
◇ Mixing bowls
◇ Saucepan of hot water
◇ Greaseproof paper
◇ Knife with a fine sharp blade

1 Place chocolate and brandy or rum in bowl over pan of hot water. Leave until melted. Beat butter with confectioner's sugar, ground almonds, egg yolks, and cocoa powder. Beat in melted chocolate, then the cookies and walnuts.

2 Turn mixture out on to a sheet of greaseproof paper. Roll paper around mixture, compacting it into a log shape about 8in (20cm) long and 3in (7.5cm) in diameter. Chill for several hours in refrigerator until set firm.

3 Unwrap the log and use knife to cut it in half diagonally.

To decorate

The chocolate log is spectacularly decorated with fine, bark-like slivers of chocolate, which partially conceal a scattering of gold-painted marzipan strips. With a stream of gold coins tumbling from its centre, the log looks as if it is bursting with treasure.

You will need

◇ 12 x 9in (30 x 23cm) cake board or flat plate
◇ 8oz (200g) plain chocolate

◇ 4oz (100g) white chocolate
◇ 4oz (100g) marzipan
◇ Gold food colouring
◇ Cocoa powder for dusting
◇ Gold-wrapped chocolate coins
◇ Marble or stone chopping board
◇ Knife with a wide sharp blade
◇ Knife for spreading
◇ Fine paint brush

1 Melt plain chocolate and pour on to marble or stone chopping board. Leave to harden. Using a knife held at an angle of 45° against the chocolate, pare off strips to resemble flaky tree bark. Use about half the chocolate; scrape up the rest and put it aside to use in step 3.

2 Roll out almond paste and cut it into fine slivers. Use paint brush to paint slivers with gold food colouring. Leave to dry.

3 Re-melt rest of plain chocolate and spread over board or plate. Position log on top. Spread dark chocolate over top and sides. Spread melted white chocolate over ends and centre of log.

4 Sprinkle cake board or plate around cake with cocoa powder. Press gold marzipan strips on to dark chocolate coat while soft, then cover log with chocolate slivers, partially concealing the marzipan. Scatter chocolate coins between cut ends of log and around it, as if they are tumbling out.

Festive cakes

Celebrations at Christmas, birthdays, weddings, christenings and anniversaries generally reach a climax with the cutting of the cake. More often than not, this is a beautiful, fancifully decorated masterpiece that provokes gasps of admiration on sight

Traditionally, festive cakes are based on a rich fruit recipe with a marzipan covering and royal icing decorations. However, some people prefer a lighter sponge cake, especially after a multicourse meal. Choosing a sponge cake makes

sense and doesn't prevent you from decorating it in an elaborate way.

Even if you haven't got the time or facilities to make your own cake, you can always buy a slab of fruit cake or a Swiss roll and decorate it beautifully yourself.

Fortunately, you don't need to be a wizard at icing to produce some really stunning effects. With a helping hand from ready-to-roll icing and bought decorations, you can easily create these eye-catching cakes. Not all the decorations have to be edible; the imaginative use of

△ *Parcel cake.*

ribbons, bows and flowers can turn a basic jelly roll into a cake fit to join the party.

Cutting an undecorated cake into an unusual shape is another quick way of creating a striking design. One diagonal cut across a square cake produces two triangular cakes, with exciting decorating possibilities. Stacking several cakes, or sections cut from the same cake, in tiers produces some equally breathtaking results.

Genoise sponge

A basic genoise sponge mixture is amazingly versatile. Bake it in a round tin for a gateau, in a square tin for modelling or in a shallow tray for rolling up into a Swiss roll.

You will need

◇ 4 medium-sized eggs
◇ Pinch of salt
◇ 4oz (120g) powdered sugar
◇ 4oz (120g) plain flour – for a chocolate sponge, substitute 1oz (30g) flour with an equal quantity of cocoa powder
◇ 1½oz (45g) unsalted butter, melted but cool

1 Heat the oven to 180°C (350°F; Gas 4). Grease and line the base and sides of the tin with greaseproof paper or baking parchment.

2 Break the eggs into a large, clean mixing bowl and add a pinch of salt and the sugar. Whisk at a medium-high speed for 5-8 minutes until the mixture is pale and fluffy and forms a continuous ribbon trail for 8-10 seconds when the whisk is lifted out.

3 Sift one-third of the flour over the mousse and fold gently into the whisked egg with a metal spoon. When nearly blended, sift in half of the remaining flour and continue folding.

4 Sift the rest of the flour over the mixture and fold in carefully until smoothly incorporated. Scrape and knock any flour clinging to the sides of the bowl into the mixture.

5 Drizzle the melted butter down the side of the bowl, folding it into the mixture as quickly and delicately as possible.

6 Pour the mixture into the tin and bake for 25-30 minutes, or according to the instructions for the different cakes.

7 Allow the sponge to stand in the tin for 5 minutes before turning out on to a wire rack. Leave to cool completely before starting to fill and decorate the cake.

Parcel cake

You will need

◇ Basic quantity of chocolate genoise sponge
◇ Larger quantity of chocolate genoise sponge, made with 6 eggs, 6oz (180g) powdered sugar, 5oz (150g) sifted flour and 1oz (30g) cocoa powder
◇ 1½ pints (900 ml) whipping cream, whipped quite firmly
◇ 1lb (480g) raspberries or raspberry jam
◇ 2lb (1kg) chocolate ready-to-roll icing
◇ 2 tbsp jam, warmed and sieved
◇ 4oz (120g) confectioner's sugar, sifted
◇ Grosgrain ribbon

1 Pour the sponge mixture into an 8in (20cm) lined tin. Bake for 25-30 minutes until the top is springy to the touch. Leave in the tin for 5 minutes before turning on to a wire rack to cool.

2 Prepare the larger genoise sponge in the same way as the basic quantity. Grease and line a 10in (25cm) square tin, pour in the sponge mixture and bake for 35-40 minutes until springy. Then cool.

3 Slice each cake in half horizon- tally through the middle. Spread each cut face with whipped cream. Arrange a layer of raspberries over the bottom half of each sponge. (If you are using raspberry jam, spread a layer over the base before spreading on the cream.) Replace the top halves over the raspberries and press down lightly to ensure they are well sandwiched together.

4 Sprinkle a light dusting of confectioner's sugar over a smooth, flat surface and roll out two square sheets of icing, one measuring 14in (35cm) square and the other 12in (30cm) square.

5 Brush the larger cake with a little melted, sieved jam and cover with the icing. Press lightly against the sides of the cake so that there are no ripples or bumps and to make it hug the contours. Trim away excess icing, leaving just enough to tuck under the base. Repeat with the smaller cake.

6 **Decorating the cake** Place the smaller cake in the centre of the bigger one. In a bowl, add

just enough warm water to the confectioner's sugar to give a smooth, stiffish coating consistency.

7 This glacé icing has to be used quickly before it begins to set or forms a crust. Spoon a little into an icing bag with a fine nozzle; pipe a swirling pattern over the surface of the stacked cakes.

8 Allow the icing pattern to dry thoroughly before tying the ribbon around the cakes, like a gift- wrapped parcel with a fancy bow.

Chocolate hazelnut meringue gateau

You will need

◇ 6 egg whites
◇ Pinch of salt
◇ 12oz (360g) powdered sugar
◇ 4oz (120g) toasted hazelnuts, finely chopped
◇ 1lb (480g) plain chocolate
◇ 1 pint (600ml) heavy cream
◇ 2 tbsp cocoa powder
◇ 2 tbsp confectioner's sugar
◇ Decorative doily or appropriate greetings stencil

1 Heat the oven to 150°C (300°F; Gas 2). Line three baking trays with non-stick baking parchment. Draw around a dessert plate to mark a 7in (18cm) circle on each.

2 Whisk the egg whites plus a pinch of salt until a stiff, white froth is formed.

3 Sprinkle the powdered sugar, a tablespoon at a time, over the egg whites while continuing to whisk fast. When all the sugar has been added, the meringue should be very stiff and snowy white.

4 Remove from the mixer and gently fold in the chopped hazelnuts, a tablespoon at a time.

5 On the baking trays, divide the meringue into three thin, flat circles using a spatula or palette knife, and bake in the oven for 75 minutes until crisp and dry. If the meringue seems to be browning too much, turn the oven down slightly, and cover with foil.

6 Allow to cool before peeling off the backing paper.

7 Using a double saucepan, melt the chocolate and cream together over water until smooth. Leave to cool before beating gently with a whisk to thicken it.

8 Assemble the gateau as near as possible to serving to keep the meringue crisp. Spread some chocolate cream evenly across the top of a meringue disc with a palette knife. Top with another disc and layer of chocolate cream, and finish with a meringue disc.

9 Cover the cake all over with the rest of the chocolate cream. Smooth off the surface with a palette knife dipped in warm water.

10 Using a sieve, sprinkle a light dusting of cocoa powder over the top of the cake. Arrange the stencil centrally on top, making sure that it masks off the rest of the cake, and dust with confectioner's sugar. Keep the gateau chilled until ready to serve.

Chocolate filigree roll

You will need
◇ Basic quantity of chocolate genoise sponge baked in a Swiss roll tin
◇ 8oz (240g) plain chocolate
◇ 8fl oz (250ml) heavy cream
◇ 8oz (240g) chocolate ready-to-roll icing
◇ 1 tbsp apricot jam, warmed and sieved
◇ 2 tbsp confectioner's sugar
◇ Stencil or doily pattern
◇ Wide ribbon

1 Thoroughly grease and line the base and sides of a shallow, rectangular tin; 13 x 9in (33 x 23cm) is suitable for a four-egg mixture. Bake for 8-10 minutes until the sponge is springy to the touch.

2 Turn the cake out on to a sheet of greaseproof paper or baking parchment. Peel off the lining paper, trim any crisp edges to straighten the sides. Roll the warm cake up along its long edge. Then unroll and repeat several times to curl the sponge as it cools.

3 Meanwhile, melt the chocolate and cream together over water in a double saucepan. Leave to cool before whisking it gently to thicken.

4 When completely cool, spread the unrolled cake with an even layer of chocolate cream. Spread the filling right up to the edges.

5 Using the paper underneath to help you, carefully roll the filled cake up as tightly as possible.

6 On a light dusting of confectioner's sugar, roll the chocolate icing out into a rectangle 18 x 8in (46 x 20cm).

7 Brush the sponge roll with a little jam. Then lift the icing over the cake with the aid of a rolling pin. Smooth it around the roll, taking care to cover the ends neatly. Trim the sheet of icing so that the two edges just overlap underneath.

8 Using a doily or a stencil, sift a lacy design in confectioner's sugar over the top of the cake. Tie a wide ribbon around the base, with an elaborate bow at one end.

◁ *Parcel cake (top), chocolate filigree roll (right) and chocolate hazelnut meringue gateau (left).*

Triangular cake

You can use this method of decorating a cake for other shapes, too. Stars and hearts, for instance, are great for celebrations or romantic occasions.

You will need

◇ 8in (20cm) square rich fruit cake, cut in half diagonally and re-joined to form a large triangle
◇ 2tbsp apricot jam, warmed and sieved
◇ 4oz (120g) ready-made marzipan
◇ 1lb (480g) ready-to-roll icing
◇ 1tbsp confectioner's sugar
◇ Silver dragées and ribbon

1 Brush the top of the cake with jam. Roll out the marzipan, lay it over the cake and trim.

2 On a light dusting of confectioner's sugar, roll out the icing. Wrap it around the cake. Make the corners as neat as you can.

3 Mix the confectioner's sugar with 1tsp water. Arrange the ribbons and silver dragées across the top, securing in place with glacé icing.

▽ *Roll of honour (top), triangular cake (right) and snow and iceball cake (left).*

Snow and iceball cake

You will need

◇ 8in (20cm) square rich fruit cake
◇ 4oz (120g) ready-made marzipan
◇ 2tbsp apricot jam, warmed and sieved
◇ 1lb (480g) ready-to-roll icing
◇ 4oz (120g) confectioner's sugar, sifted
◇ 3ft (1m) satin ribbon, 2in (5cm) wide
◇ Silver dragées and ribbon

1 Sprinkle some confectioner's sugar on a flat surface and roll out the marzipan into an 8in (20cm) square to fit the top of the cake.

2 Brush the top of the cake with jam and smooth the marzipan over the top, trimming to fit.

3 On a light dusting of confectioner's sugar, roll out the icing into a 12in (30cm) square.

4 Brush the surface of the cake and marzipan lightly with jam. Lift up the icing around the rolling pin, place it over the cake and press against the sides. Trim at the base.

5 Wind the ribbon tightly around the cake, with the bottom edge about a third of the way up. Brush the overlapping ends of the ribbon with glacé icing and press together firmly until

completely dry. To make a stiff glacé icing, mix 2tbsp confectioner's sugar with 1-2tsp water.

6 Dip one side of a silver dragée into the glacé icing and press against the icing around the base of the cake. Repeat all the way round, then build up further rows until the silver baubles reach the bottom of the ribbon. Fix one or two rows of dragées above the ribbon.

7 Dust the top of the cake heavily with confectioner's sugar. Arrange a silver dragée and ribbon pattern over the sugar.

Roll of honour

You will need

◇ Bought jam or chocolate Swiss roll
◇ 6oz (180g) ready-to-roll icing
◇ 1 tbsp apricot jam, warmed and sieved
◇ 2tbsp confectioner's sugar
◇ Silver dragées and ribbon

1 Roll out the icing. Brush the Swiss roll with jam and wrap the icing round the cake, pressing it neatly over the curves and ends.

2 Devise a geometric pattern using the silver dragées, ribbon and confectioner's sugar, attaching them with some stiff glacé icing made as in step 5.

Miniature cakes

*Miniature cakes, attractively packaged in small
gift boxes, make charming presents and can be decorated to suit
any occasion from birthdays and anniversaries to
Christmas and Easter. Choose from the stunning designs featured
here or create your own personalized versions.*

The perfect base for miniature cakes is a rich fruit cake laced with plenty of brandy. Use a tried and tested recipe and add extra flavour by drizzling the cakes with a little more brandy after cooking. If preferred, a rich sponge cake makes an equally effective base.

Both the round and the square cakes measure 3in (7.5cm), which allows sufficient space for an attractive, eye-catching design. Keep the designs simple but effective, being careful to avoid a cluttered or clumsy look caused by too much decoration or overly large motifs. Small metal crimpers and cutters (available from most kitchenware shops) are ideal for miniature cakes and can be used to produce a range of effects.

Baking tins

For small round cakes, make baking tins from empty food cans. Remove both ends from a small can about 3in (7.5cm) in diameter. Wash thoroughly and dry. Place on a baking sheet and line with greaseproof paper as you would a large cake tin. Collect several empty cans if baking more than one round mini cake.

For small square cakes, simply use four (or more) times the amount of cake mixture needed to make one small cake, and bake the whole in a large square baking tin; leave the cake to cool, then remove it from the tin and cut it into four (or more) small square cakes.

Cake mixture quantities

Use cake mixture for a 6in (15cm) square cake to make four square or six round mini cakes; mixture for a 9in (23cm) square cake makes nine square or twelve round mini cakes.

Preparing the cakes

Each cake is covered with marzipan and plain or coloured moulding icing, which provides the ideal base for all kinds of decorative effects. A cake crimper is used to produce a scalloped finish around the base of the cakes.

You will need
◇ 3in (7.5cm) round or square rich fruit cake
◇ 4in (10cm) round or square silver or gold cake board
◇ 4oz (100g) marzipan
◇ 4oz (100g) moulding icing, coloured as desired
◇ Cornflour
◇ Small sharp knife
◇ Metal cake crimpers

1 Place cake on cake board. Cover with marzipan (see pages 8-9) and then moulding icing (see pages 32-33).

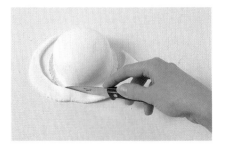

2 Press icing around base of cake. Use knife to trim excess, leaving an ⅛in (3mm) lip of icing around base. Keep trimmings for cake decorations.

3 Lightly dust ends of crimpers with cornflour. Holding ends of crimpers ¼in (6mm) apart, lightly squeeze lip of icing around base of cake to give decorative scalloped finish all round cake.

Christmas cake

A miniature fruit cake decorated with seasonal motifs and a bright red ribbon is the perfect Christmas present. The relief design is formed with a delicate holly-shaped cutter, pressed over the surface of the cake, then coloured with food dyes.

You will need
◇ Small, round white-iced cake with crimped base (see above)
◇ Small, holly-shaped cutter
◇ Cornflour
◇ Fine paint brush
◇ Green and red food colouring
◇ Moulding icing trimmings
◇ Thin red ribbon

1 Dip holly-shaped cutter in cornflour and gently press single and grouped leaf shapes into icing on cake.

2 Dilute a little green food colouring with water and use fine brush strokes to paint holly shapes. Paint from the centre of the leaf out towards the edges.

3 Colour icing trimmings red and green and shape small parcels. Arrange on cake and secure with dampened brush. Roll tiny pieces of red icing for holly berries, and arrange next to leaves. Tie ribbon around base to finish.

TIP	CUTTERS

◇ Use cutters and crimpers soon after icing the cake, while the icing is pliable.

◇ Practise the technique on a spare piece of icing first.

Parcel cake

This small square cake is covered with soft peach moulding icing and decorated with delicate scattered blossoms to create the impression of printed wrapping paper. Pink ribbon and flowers complete the look.

You will need
◇ Small, square peach-iced cake (see opposite)
◇ Small, blossom-shaped cutter
◇ Cornflour
◇ Fine paint brush
◇ Peach food colouring
◇ Thin pink ribbon
◇ Pale pink or peach silk flowers
◇ Small quantity of royal icing (see page 12)

1 Dip blossom cutter into cornflour and gently press scattered blossom shapes into moulding icing. Using a fine paint brush and thinned peach food colouring, paint centres of blossoms.

2 Cut two strips of thin pink ribbon to fit over top and sides of cake as shown; secure ribbon with dots of icing. To finish, add bow and a cluster of silk flowers with dots of royal icing.

Garland cake

Small cakes can look just as elegant and sophisticated as larger ones. This ivory cake is decorated with garlands of deep blue icing and delicate cut-out blossoms, with gold dragées for a luxurious touch.

You will need
◇ Small, round ivory-iced cake with crimped base (see opposite)
◇ Small, blossom-shaped cutter
◇ Cornflour
◇ Ivory moulding icing trimmings
◇ Blue food colouring
◇ Paint brush
◇ Gold dragées
◇ Piping bag with fine nozzle
◇ Small quantity royal icing (see page 12)
◇ Small, pale blue candle

1 Colour half of moulding icing trimmings deep blue and roll out on cornfloured surface. Cut icing into four thin strips, 3½in (9cm) long. Carefully twist strips and loop around sides of cake as shown. To secure, dampen ends and press them on to cake.

2 Dip blossom cutter in cornflour and cut out several blossoms from remaining ivory icing trimmings. Press small candle into centre of cake and scatter small blossoms around it, securing them to cake with dampened paint brush. Place a blossom at each of the four joins of the blue garland.

3 Pipe a dot of royal icing into centre of some blossoms, including those joining garland loops, and press in a gold dragée.

Valentine cake

Surprise a loved one with this charming miniature Valentine cake. To decorate the cake, simply scatter a few heart motifs across its surface and finish with a bright red icing gift tag. Many cutters, like the heart shapes used here, come in two or more sizes which can be used together on a cake for a simple but effective design. Delicate red bows attached to the sides of the cake complete the look.

You will need
◇ Small, square white-iced cake, with crimped base (see opposite)
◇ Small heart-shaped cutters in two sizes
◇ Cornflour
◇ Moulding icing trimmings
◇ Red food colouring
◇ Fine paint brush
◇ Sharp knife
◇ Cocktail stick
◇ Thin red ribbon

1 Dip heart-shaped cutters into cornflour and gently press different sized heart shapes into icing on cake. Use thinned red food colouring and fine brush to paint centres of heart shapes.

2 Colour icing trimmings red and roll out on cornfloured surface. Use knife to cut out a larger heart

shape for gift tag. With cocktail stick, make hole at top of heart for threading ribbon. Leave to harden for 24 hours.

3 Thread piece of ribbon through tag and tie with bow. Place tag on cake, propped up against a small ball of white icing. Finish cake with extra bows.

Child's birthday cake

A personalized miniature birthday cake will delight a young child. Add the appropriate number of candles and choose decorations to suit the recipient — our railway theme is perfect for a young train fanatic.

You will need
◇ Small, square white-iced cake, with crimped base (see page 90)
◇ Brown food colouring
◇ Fine paint brush
◇ Moulding icing trimmings
◇ Small plastic train
◇ Colourful ribbon
◇ Small candle(s)

Use the fine paint brush and thinned brown food colouring to paint a railway track across the top of the cake. Add the appropriate number of candles in the corner of the cake, and attach the train at the end of the track with a small blob of icing. Attach ribbon around the cake to finish it off.

Marzipan fruit cake
The fruit decorations for this colourful cake are made from coloured and moulded marzipan. The cake takes a little longer to complete than the others, but the result is stunning.

You will need
◇ Small, round yellow-iced cake, with crimped base (see page 90)
◇ Marzipan
◇ Selection of food colourings for marzipan fruits
◇ Fine paint brush
◇ Cloves for marzipan oranges
◇ Thin green ribbon

Make the miniature marzipan fruits as described on page 45. Arrange and secure the fruits on top of the cake using dampened paint brush. To finish, tie green ribbon around the cake.

Presenting the cakes
Present the miniature cakes attractively packaged in small gift boxes. Transparent display boxes can sometimes be found in kitchenware shops and are perfect for showing off small cakes — use colourful ribbons and bows to brighten them up.

Alternatively, collect empty gift boxes and cover them with pretty wrapping paper. Empty patterned or plain coloured boxes can also be bought in stationers and stores with good paperware departments. If the boxes are larger than required, line them with crumpled tissue paper in a matching colour.

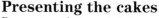

◁ *Gift-wrap the miniature cakes to make presents with a personal touch. Choose a box to suit the style of your cake and decorate it with colourful ribbons and bows.*

Christmas cookies

*Celebrate Christmas with an eye-catching selection
of festive cookies, which can be hung from your tree, served
as seasonal treats or giftwrapped and presented to
friends. Decorate the cookies with raised motifs and swirls
of piped royal icing, and paint them in bright colours.*

The festive cookies are made from a traditional spicy cookie recipe, and colourfully decorated with a smooth icing glaze and piped royal icing. Raised designs, like the holly leaves, Christmas stocking and star, are created with superimposed marzipan or cookie dough cut-outs, and painted for extra emphasis.

Make the cookies about 2¼in (6cm) in diameter to allow enough space for a design. Simple decorative shapes and motifs look effective and are easiest to manage.

For the best flavour and texture, do not make the cookies too far in advance. Once iced and decorated, they will keep well in an airtight tin for up to one week. If hung on the Christmas tree, they are best eaten after one or two days.

To make cookie dough

This spicy cookie recipe is ideal for festive cookies, as it is full of flavour without being too sweet — an important consideration as the cookies have a sweet icing.

You will need
For about 25 cookies
◇ 6oz (150g) plain flour
◇ 2tsp ground mixed spice
◇ 4oz (100g) butter
◇ 1½oz (40g) light brown sugar
◇ 1 egg yolk
◇ A little cold water
◇ Mixing bowl
◇ Sieve

Sift the flour and spice into bowl. Add butter, broken into small pieces, and rub it into the mixture with your fingertips. Stir in sugar and egg yolk. Mix well, adding a little cold water to make a firm dough.

Remove dough from bowl and knead lightly. Chill until needed.

To make icing glaze

The baked and cooled cookies are topped with a white icing glaze which, once dry, provides a perfect background for painting designs with brightly coloured food dyes.

You will need
◇ 1 egg white

Christmas stocking and holly cookies

The raised Christmas motifs on these cookies are created with cut-out marzipan shapes, mounted on the cookies, then glazed and painted in bright, festive colours. Even quite delicate marzipan cut-outs, like the fine, pointed outlines of the holly leaves, hold their shape and remain well-defined under the icing glaze.

You will need
◇ Quantity spicy cookie mixture
◇ Icing glaze
◇ Royal icing for piping
◇ 4oz (100g) marzipan
◇ Red, green and yellow food colouring
◇ Plain or fluted circular biscuit cutter, 2¼in (6cm) in diameter
◇ Small holly-shaped cutter
◇ Fine-bladed knife
◇ Skewer or cocktail stick
◇ Fine paint brush
◇ Fine ribbon
◇ Icing bag fitted with a fine writer nozzle

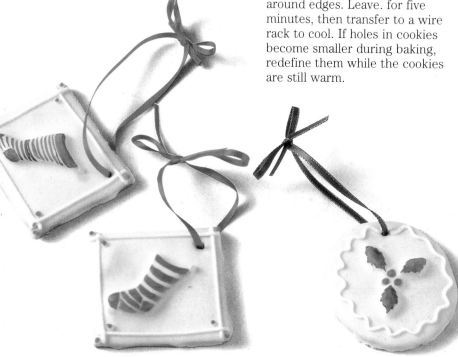

1 Roll out cookie mixture. Use knife to cut out rectangles about 2¾ x 2¼in (7 x 6cm) from one half of mixture. Use circular cutter to cut out circles from other half. With skewer or cocktail stick, make a hole in each cookie, ¼in (6mm) in from its edge, for threading ribbon.

2 Place cookies on greased baking sheet and bake at 180°C (325°F; Gas 4) for 12-15 minutes, or until they are golden around edges. Leave. for five minutes, then transfer to a wire rack to cool. If holes in cookies become smaller during baking, redefine them while the cookies are still warm.

3 Roll out the marzipan and use holly-shaped cutter to cut out holly leaves. Cut out stocking shapes using a knife, either free-hand or using a stencil (see Santa Claus biscuits on page 96). Make small holly berries from marzipan trimmings. Position stocking cut-outs on the rectangular cookies, and three holly leaf cut-outs on each circular cookie. Place berries in centre of holly leaves. Secure marzipan trimmings with a little icing glaze if necessary.

4 Space cookies slightly apart on a cooling rack. Spoon icing glaze over cookies and use paint brush to spread it in a smooth, even layer. Leave glaze to harden for several hours or overnight.

◇ 1tbsp lemon juice
◇ 4oz (100g) confectioner's sugar, sifted
◇ Mixing bowl

Pour egg white and lemon juice into bowl. Gradually beat in confectioner's sugar until mixture thinly coats the back of a metal tablespoon. To prevent a crust forming, cover surface of icing glaze with cling film until needed.

To make piped icing

A basic royal icing is used to pipe designs over the cookie surfaces.

You will need
◇ 1 egg white
◇ 8oz (200g) confectioner's sugar, sifted

Gradually beat confectioner's sugar into egg white until mixture just holds its shape. Cover with cling film until needed.

TIP	FREEZING

To save time, prepare the cookie mixture and cut out the shapes in advance; then interleave the cookies with greaseproof paper and place them in the freezer until needed for baking.

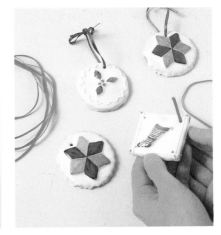

5 Put royal icing in piping bag and pipe a wavy border around circular cookies and straight border around rectangular cookies, about ¹/₄in (6mm) in from edges. Complete rectangular border with small piped dots in corners.

6 Once the piped borders have hardened, paint the raised motifs using a fine paint brush and food colouring thinned with a little water. Leave to dry.

7 Once dry, thread fine ribbon through holes in cookies and tie bows for hanging.

Star cookies

The striking raised star design on these cookies is created simply by superimposing an additional shaped layer of cookie dough on the cookie base before baking; the baked cookie is then glazed and painted. This technique is particularly effective for large designs in simple shapes.

You will need
◇ Quantity spicy cookie mixture
◇ Icing glaze
◇ Food colouring in bright colours
◇ Plain or fluted circular cookie cutter, 2¹/₄in (6cm) in diameter
◇ Star-shaped cutter, 1¹/₂-2in (4-5cm) in diameter
◇ Skewer or cocktail stick
◇ Fine paint brush
◇ Fine ribbon

1 Roll out the cookie mixture. Use a circular cutter to cut out shapes from two-thirds of the mixture. With star-shaped cutter, cut out stars from the remaining third of the mixture. Place a star in the centre of each cookie circle. Make a hole in each cookie and bake as described in steps 1 and 2 of the stocking and holly cookies. Once baked, leave cookies to cool on a wire rack.

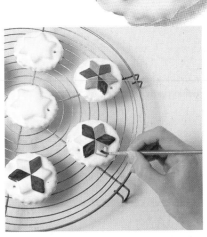

2 Cover cookies with icing glaze and leave to harden. Paint raised star designs with two shades of thinned food colouring. Leave to dry, then thread with ribbon and tie bows for hanging.

Santa Claus cookies

These skating Santa Claus cookies are cut from the template given right, then baked and decorated with brightly coloured, piped royal icing. The piped icing is slightly stiffer than the icing glaze. Use this template or design your own the glowing candle in the main picture was made this way.

Santa Claus template

You will need
◇ Quantity spicy cookie mixture
◇ Royal icing for piping
◇ Red food colouring
◇ 2oz (50g) plain chocolate
◇ Greaseproof paper for template
◇ Pencil
◇ Scissors
◇ Fine-bladed knife
◇ Three paper icing bags, one fitted with fine writer nozzle
◇ Saucepan of hot water
◇ Medium-sized bowl

1 Trace the Santa Claus template on to greaseproof paper and cut out. Roll out cookie mixture, place template on it and use knife tip to cut out 10-12 shapes. Bake as described in step 2 of holly and stocking cookies. Cool.

2 Colour half royal icing red and place in an icing bag. Cut ⅛in (3mm) off tip of bag. Use icing to fill Santa Claus's red coat and hat, adding a small red dot for nose; pipe three or four extra lines of icing over body to resemble arms. Put white icing in separate bag, snip off end and use icing to pipe beard, moustache, hat and coat trimmings and skate blades.

3 Break up chocolate and place in bowl over saucepan of hot water, until melted. Spoon into piping bag fitted with fine writer nozzle and use to pipe the eyes and skating boots of the Santa Claus. Leave cookies so that the icing hardens for 1-2 hours.

Fruit and nut cookies

For quick but equally stunning results, coat some basic cookie shapes in a brightly coloured icing glaze and decorate them with nuts and dried or glacé fruit pieces.

You will need
◇ Quantity spicy cookie mixture
◇ Icing glaze
◇ Yellow food colouring
◇ Selection of nuts (halved if too large), such as pistachios, almonds, cashews, walnuts and coconut flakes
◇ Selection of dried and glacé fruits (chopped if too large), such as cherries, apricots, sultanas and pineapple
◇ Crescent-shaped cutter
◇ Fine-bladed knife
◇ Tablespoon

1 Roll out cookie mixture. Use cutter to cut out several crescent shapes and knife to cut out small triangles. Bake as described in step 2 of holly and stocking cookies. Leave to cool on wire rack. Colour icing glaze yellow and spoon over cookies.

2 While icing is still soft, press a colourful selection of fruits and nuts on to cookies. Leave to harden for 1-2 hours.

Iced petit fours

Transform a plain sponge cake – bought or home-made – into sophisticated, mouthwatering petit fours. Served with coffee and liqueurs, these miniature iced cakes are perfect for tempting the palate at the end of a normal meal.

With just a little time and patience you can turn a few basic ingredients into professional-looking petit fours. Use a bought or home-made sponge about ³/₄in (2cm) deep and, to add extra flavour, drizzle it with a little brandy or liqueur before icing. It is not essential to add liquid glucose to the icing mixture as described in the instructions but it does help the icing to 'coat' more easily and gives it a more professional finish with an attractive sheen. Iced petit fours will keep for up to a week, stored in an airtight tin in a cool place.

You will need
◇ Shallow sponge cake, about 7in (18cm) square
◇ 2tbsp apricot jam
◇ 4oz (100g) marzipan
◇ 1tbsp liquid glucose
◇ 12oz (350g) confectioner's sugar, sifted
◇ Pastel food colourings of your choice

To finish
◇ 1 egg white
◇ 8oz (200g) confectioner's sugar, sifted
◇ Piping bag with a fine writer nozzle
◇ Miniature paper cases

1 Heat the jam gently and rub it through a sieve. Brush it on to the top of the cake. Lightly knead the marzipan, then roll it out thinly to the same dimensions as the cake. Lift it over the cake and press it down lightly to secure, using your fingertips.

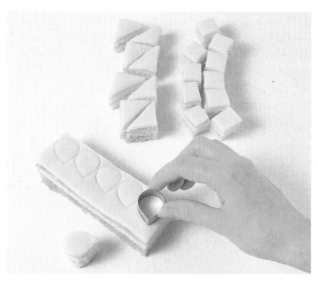

2 Cut cake into small round, square or triangular shapes. Rounds and squares should be ³/₄in (2cm) in diameter. Use a small petit four cutter for the rounds. To make the triangular shapes, cut 1¹/₄in (3cm) squares and cut these in half diagonally.

3 Put the liquid glucose into a pan with 5tbsp water and heat very gently. Add sifted confectioner's sugar, stirring until mixture is smooth and thickly coats the back of the spoon when lifted out of the mixture.

◆ TIP	CHOCOLATE

For added colour and contrast, use melted chocolate to decorate some of the petit fours. Place the melted chocolate in the piping bag and decorate as above.

4 Place petit fours on a cooling rack over a large plate or tray. Using a tablespoon, pour a little icing over each cake so that it runs down to cover the top and sides completely. To make coloured icing, put a little icing in a separate bowl and beat in a few drops of food colouring. Leave cakes for at least one hour to allow the icing to harden before adding the final decorative touches.

5 To finish, beat egg white with the extra confectioner's sugar until icing just holds its shape. Using a piping bag fitted with a fine writer nozzle, pipe decorative dots, lines or spirals on to iced cakes.

6 Leave cakes for a further hour to harden. Then, use a knife to lift petit fours off cooling rack and transfer them to the paper petit four cases.

Dainty petit fours

*From chewy chocolate florentines to prettily
stuffed fruits, delicious yet delicate petit fours are thoroughly
enjoyable to make at home. This fruit and
nut selection is perfect for rounding off a dinner party
or any other special occasion.*

Any sweet, delicately-sized morsel served with coffee may be called a petit four. They include dainty iced cakes, cookies and chocolates, and are usually served after a special meal.

The following recipes are all based on nuts or dried fruit and include some of the petit four classics, such as macaroons. Most petit fours can be made several days in advance, provided they are placed in a single layer in an airtight container, in a cool place. The florentine cookies, macaroons and filling for the chocolate and apricot wedges can be made a week in advance and finished nearer the day. For more petit four recipes, see pages 97-98 and 103-106.

Materials and equipment

Metal cases Miniature, boat-shaped metal cases are needed to shape some of the petit four cases. They come in various shapes and are useful for moulding chocolate.

Paper cases Use small paper petit four or sweet cases to present the petit fours. These can also be used as moulds for the chocolate

as an alternative to the metal cases. They are available from kitchenware shops, stationers, and occasionally from larger supermarkets.

You will also need a baking tray, cooling rack and piping bag with star and plain nozzles.

Glazed fruits

These tempting dried fruit morsels are stuffed with home-made marzipan and decorated with pistachio nuts, then coated with a glistening syrup glaze.

You will need
For 20 fruits
◇ 20 no-need-to-soak dried apricots or pitted prunes
◇ 2oz (50g) ground almonds, hazelnuts or walnuts
◇ loz (25g) powdered sugar
◇ ltbsp beaten egg white
◇ Small sharp knife

To finish
◇ 10 shelled and skinned pistachio nuts
◇ 2tbsp maple syrup or honey
◇ Fine paint brush

1 Make a slit with a sharp knife through to the centre of each apricot or prune so that the cavities can be filled.

2 Beat together the ground nuts, sugar and egg white to make a stiff paste. Roll into a thin sausage and cut into 20 even sized pieces. Roll into oval shapes and tuck one into each fruit.

3 Just before serving, decorate the fruits with halved pistachio nuts and paint them with syrup or a glaze of clear honey.

Coconut rolled fruits

A dried fruit paste is steeped in liqueur, then rolled into balls and coated in toasted coconut to make a rich and tipsy treat.

You will need
For about 30 fruits
◇ 12oz (350g) mixture of dried fruit such as dates, figs, pears, apricots, sultanas
◇ 3tbsp of orange flavoured liqueur such as Cointreau or Grand Marnier
◇ 2oz (50g) desiccated coconut, toasted

1 Roughly chop the fruit and place in a bowl. Cover fruit with the liqueur and leave for at least two hours. Once the fruit has been steeped, blend to a paste in a food processor.

2 Roll the mixture into small balls about ³/₄in (2cm) in diameter. Roll them in coconut.

Mini florentines

These little cookies are made with a rich fruit and nut mixture. They are topped with a layer of plain chocolate, marked into a distinctive swirl.

You will need
For about 24 florentines
◇ ltbsp each of flaked almonds and chopped walnuts
◇ 2tbsp chopped glacé cherries
◇ tbsp chopped mixed dried fruit
◇ 1¹/₂oz (40g) powdered sugar
◇ 2tbsp plain flour
◇ ¹/₂oz (15g) butter, melted
◇ 2in (5cm) metal cutter, lightly oiled

To finish
◇ 2oz (50g) plain chocolate, melted

Work quickly once the cookies are out of the oven. They firm up in 1-2 minutes and become difficult to shape. To avoid this, bake the cookies in small quantities. Should cookies harden too rapidly, return them to oven briefly; this should soften them sufficiently.

Chocolate and apricot wedges

A dried apricot paste is soaked in brandy and rolled into balls, which are then flattened into a small 'cake' shape. The cake is dipped in plain chocolate and cut into bite-sized wedges.

You will need
For about 16 wedges

◇ 8oz (225g) no-need-to-soak dried apricots
◇ 3tbsp brandy
◇ 4oz (100g) plain chocolate

1 Preheat the oven to 375°F (190°C; Gas 5). Beat together the fruit, nuts, sugar, flour and butter. Place half teaspoonsful of the mixture on to baking sheet, spaced well apart, and bake for 5-7 minutes until the cookies spread.

1 Roughly chop the apricots and place them in a bowl with the brandy. Leave to steep for at least two hours. Blend to a paste in a food processor. Divide the mixture into four pieces. Shape each piece into a ball, then flatten into a little 'cake' shape. Chill until the mixture is firm.

2 Swirl the metal cutter around each spread cookie, bringing mixture into centre to shape into a neat cookie about 1½in (4cm) in diameter. Transfer to a wire rack to cool. Re-grease baking sheet and cook remaining mixture as described in step 1.

2 Dip each apricot cake in melted chocolate, spreading chocolate over cake with a knife. Transfer to a wire rack and chill until the chocolate has hardened. Cut each one into quarters.

3 Once cooled, spread flat undersides of cookies with the chocolate and make a swirled finish with a fork. Leave to set.

◆ To skin pistachio nuts, place them in a bowl with a little boiling water for two minutes. The skin is then easy to rub away.

◆ If fruit mixture is difficult to handle, wet hands slightly before rolling mixture into balls.

Chocolate cream boats

These delicate plain chocolate boats are filled with an exquisite piped mixture of white chocolate and cream, then dusted with cocoa powder. Each boat contains an almond hidden beneath the filling.

You will need
For about 16 boats
◇ 4oz (100g) plain chocolate, melted
◇ 16 whole blanched almonds
◇ 2oz (50g) white chocolate, melted
◇ 3fl oz (75ml) heavy cream
◇ Cocoa powder for dusting
◇ Small metal petit four moulds
◇ Piping bag fitted with a small star nozzle
◇ Sharp knife

1 Using a knife, line the metal moulds with the melted plain chocolate. Thickly coat the moulds so that the cases are easy to remove. Chill until the chocolate has hardened.

2 Use the tip of a sharp knife to loosen the chocolate from the moulds. Place an almond in the centre of each case.

3 Whip the cream and beat in the white chocolate until mixture is stiff enough to pipe. Place in the piping bag and pipe swirls of cream into chocolate cases. Dust lightly with cocoa powder.

Macaroons

The macaroons are sandwiched together with a smooth, rich mixture of melted chocolate and cream, which contrasts well with the flavour of the cookies.

You will need
For 12 macaroons
◇ 3oz (75g) ground almonds (use walnuts or hazelnuts, if you prefer)
◇ 2 egg whites
◇ 1½oz (40g) powdered sugar
◇ Lightly greased baking sheet
◇ Piping bag fitted with a ⅓in (1cm) star-shaped piping nozzle

To finish
◇ 3oz (75g) plain chocolate, melted
◇ 2fl oz (50ml) heavy cream
◇ Piping bag fitted with a small star nozzle

1 Preheat the oven to 350°F (180°C; Gas 4). Place the nuts and sugar in a bowl. Add the egg whites and mix to a soft paste. Place in piping bag and use to pipe small rounds, about ¾in (2cm) in diameter on to the baking sheet. Use a knife to slice off the paste from the piping nozzle once the round is the correct diameter.

2 Bake macaroons for about 15 minutes until they begin to colour. Transfer them to a wire rack to cool.

3 Beat chocolate with cream until firm. Pipe swirls over flat sides of half the cookies. Sandwich with remaining cookies.

▽ *These tempting treats will impress any dinner guest, yet they are simple to make.*

Mini meringues

*Crisp morsels of melt-in-the mouth meringue
make pretty and delicious sweets. Colour the meringue or
sculpt it into unpredictable shapes and serve these
treats with a refreshing fruit salad or compote, or simply to
accompany after-dinner coffee.*

Making meringues

Meringues are made by combining just two ingredients — egg whites and sugar. The secret to perfecting this seemingly simple desert lies in the way it is whisked and by adding the sugar with great care.

A smoother, less aerated mixture is needed for the small meringues shown here, than is required for large meringue desserts. The reason for this is that the meringue must be able to hold its shape even when it is piped with a fine nozzle.

Equipment

The bowl, glass or copper is best, and the **whisk,** must be clean and free from grease.

Large nylon or greaseproof bags for piping, which will be able to hold the bulky mixture.

Plain and star nozzles were used for these meringues.

Bakewell parchment paper is best for covering the baking sheets as it is less likely to stick to the meringue than greaseproof paper.

Pastel paper cake cases can be used to present small meringues.

Basic meringue mixture

This quantity makes 40 to 50 individual meringues.

You will need

◇ Two egg whites
◇ 2³/₄oz (69g) confectioner's sugar, sifted

1 Place egg whites and all the confectioner's sugar in a clean, grease-free bowl and whisk them lightly until combined thoroughly.

2 Place bowl over a saucepan containing hot, not boiling water, and whisk until the mixture is stiff and forms peaks when whisk is lifted from the bowl.

3 Remove bowl from the heat and continue to whisk until the bowl is cool and the mixture forms very stiff, glossy peaks.

4 For contrasting colour or flavour, spoon a little of the meringue into a separate bowl. Add either a few drops of dissolved instant coffee, cocoa powder or pink or green food colouring. Fold colour or flavouring in carefully, until meringue is no longer streaky.

Shaping meringue

Choose from the following ideas for making pretty decorative meringues. The mixture given makes 40 to 50 mini meringues, so make a whole batch of one shape, or divide the mixture and try several different ideas. All will keep for up to three weeks in an airtight tin, provided cream has not been added to decorate.

Preparation

Before starting to pipe, line several baking sheets with bakewell parchment. Secure the paper in place with a blob of meringue to prevent the paper slipping.

Cooking

Preheat the oven to the lowest setting available on your oven – 110°C/225°F/Gas¹/₄. Cook meringues on lower shelves for 2-3 hours, leaving oven door slightly ajar if the meringues start to colour.

Meringue mushrooms

Mushroom shapes are easy to pipe in meringue. They are made in two stages and once the top is dusted with cocoa powder, the effect is quite convincing.

1 Place meringue in a piping bag that has been fitted with a ½in (1.2cm) plain nozzle.

2 For caps, pipe blobs of about 1in (2.5cm) in diameter on to paper. Release meringue by sliding a knife under the nozzle. For stems, pipe a blob of meringue in the same way, then without squeezing bag, pull upwards until meringue breaks off in a point. Bake as given.

3 To assemble, lightly dust caps with cocoa powder. Press tip of stems into bases of caps. If meringue is very firm, first make a hole in the base with a skewer — then position caps.

Cream swans

These serene swans, with a luscious cream filling, will delight small children — and adults too! First pipe the sides and necks of the swans, then join them together with lashings of cream.

1 Place meringue in a piping bag fitted with a ¼in (5mm) plain nozzle, or snip off the corner of a greaseproof bag. Pipe 'S' shapes, about 2¼in (6cm) long on to paper, finishing with a point at head end.

2 For wings, pipe a scroll shape on to paper. Pipe a second slightly larger scroll, touching the first one. Pipe the third scroll slightly larger again. Pipe an equal quantity of wings, remembering to reverse half the shapes to make pairs of wings. Bake as given.

3 To assemble, pipe whipped cream on to greaseproof paper, then gently press wings to each side of cream. Rest swan neck in cream to finish. Present swans sitting in a paper case if desired.

Meringue flowers

These flowers have been coloured and flavoured with coffee. The 'petals' are piped first, then the centre is added. Try tinting the meringue with food colouring for pretty, pastel flowers.

1 Flavour a little meringue with coffee and place in piping bag fitted with a ¼in (5mm) nozzle or a greasproof bag with a corner snipped off.

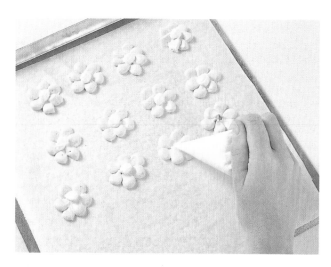

2 Pipe a rosette of six small blobs on to paper, drawing the points into centre. Finish with a white blob in the centre. Make more flowers with white rosettes and coffee centres. Bake as given.

Hazelnut twists

A crunchy hazelnut, hidden inside the meringue makes a surprise bite. The meringue is literally piped around the nut, then baked.

1 Place meringue in a piping bag fitted with a large star nozzle. Pipe 'stars' of meringue on to paper and top each with a hazelnut. Pipe swirls of meringue around and over the nut to completely enclose it. Bake as given.

Pastel creams

Delicious meringues look even more mouth-watering when tinted a pale pastel shade. Sandwich the meringues together with cream and present them in a pastel paper cake case.

1 Carefully colour meringue pale pink or green and place it in a piping bag fitted with a ½in (1.2cm) plain nozzle. Pipe small blobs of meringue on to paper. Bake as given.

2 When cooled sandwich together in pairs with a little cream or drizzle with glacé icing.

Magnificent meringues

All meringue is a snow-like fantasy whisked out of egg whites and sugar.
It can be spread out into flat rounds, spooned into small dollops or piped,
with a plain or fluted nozzle, into far more elaborate scrolls, fingers and nests.

There are basically two ways of cooking meringue. It can be dried out in a very cool oven to form a crisp, white shell (be sure to pipe or spread the meringue mixture on to non-stick silicone paper for easy release after baking); or it can be cooked far more quickly at a higher temperature to remain as a soft topping.

When whipping meringue, it is crucial to make sure that the bowl in which you whisk the egg whites is absolutely clean and grease free. A glass, metal or china bowl is easier to wash thoroughly than a plastic one. To avoid getting the tiniest scrap of egg yolk into the whites, separate the eggs one by one into smaller bowls, then transfer the whites to the mixing bowl.

Meringue is versatile. For instance, a Pavlova is an eccentric variation on the basic meringue mix – it has a soupçon of vinegar and cornflour added to produce a crisp crust over a marshmallowy centre. Meringue can even do the seemingly impossible by protecting ice cream in a baked Alaska during cooking. All the tiny air bubbles trapped in the whipped egg whites act as insulators to prevent the ice cream melting.

Sandwich two meringue shells with whipped cream for a melt-in-the-mouth partnership. Meringue with ice-cream and fruit accompaniment makes and enticing, summery dessert. Dip the base of a dried meringue shell in melted chocolate, or drizzle a little across the top, for a luxurious effect. Vary the flavour of the uncooked meringue mixture by folding in some chopped nuts or cocoa powder or whisking in some coffee essence.

Crisp meringues can be stored in an airtight container for at least a week. Crush the last of the batch into whipped cream with some fresh fruit for a scrumptious quick dessert.

▽ *Strawberry passion fruit Pavlova.*

Strawberry and passion fruit Pavlova

You will need
◇ 3 egg whites
◇ 6oz (180g) powdered sugar
◇ 1 tsp vinegar
◇ 1 tbsp cornflour
◇ ½ tsp vanilla essence
◇ ½pt (300ml) whipping cream
◇ 8oz (240g) strawberries
◇ 2 passion fruits

1 Heat the oven to 140°C (275°F; Gas 1). Line a baking sheet with a sheet of silicone non-stick paper. Mark a circle on the paper by drawing round an 8in (20cm) plate.

2 Whisk the egg whites until the froth forms soft peaks.

3 Add the sugar a tablespoon at a time while continuing to whisk. Add the vinegar, cornflour and vanilla essence to the meringue with the last spoonful of sugar.

4 Spread the meringue mixture over the marked circle on the baking tray. Use a plastic spatula or the back of a spoon to raise the sides higher than the centre.

5 Place in the centre of the oven and bake for 1 hour until the crust is crisp and the meringue has turned a pale cream colour.

6 Turn the oven off and leave the Pavlova inside to cool down completely. Then carefully ease it off the paper on to a flat serving plate.

7 Whip the cream until it forms stiff peaks and spread it into the central hollow of the Pavlova.

8 Cut the strawberries into quarters. Slit the passion fruits in half, scoop the seeds into a sieve and press out as much juice as possible over the strawberries. Stir well before piling high on top of the whipped cream.

9 Keep in the refrigerator until ready to serve. A Pavlova's arrival at the table provides a sensational climax to any meal.

Nectarine meringue gateau

△ *Nectarine meringue gateau.*

You will need
◇ 6 egg whites
◇ 12oz (360g) powdered sugar
◇ 16fl oz (500ml) whipping cream
◇ 6 ripe nectarines, cut into slices

1 Heat the oven to 110°C (225°F; Gas ¼). Line three baking trays with silicone non-stick baking parchment and mark 8in (20cm) circles on each tray.

2 Whisk the egg whites until the froth forms soft peaks.

3 Gradually add the sugar, a tablespoon at a time while continuing to whisk fast, until a stiff meringue is formed.

4 Spoon the meringue into a piping bag fitted with a ¾in (2cm) plain nozzle. Starting in the centre of each circle marked on the baking parchment, pipe round in an even, continuous spiral until three flat coils of meringue fill the discs.

Pineapple meringue swans

You will need
◇ 3 egg whites
◇ 6oz (180g) powdered sugar
◇ ½pt (300ml) whipping cream
◇ 1 fresh pineapple, with the core removed and cut into 8 thin slices
◇ Strawberries for garnish

1 Heat the oven to 110°C (225°F; Gas ¼). Line a large baking sheet with silicone non-stick baking parchment.

2 Whisk the egg whites until the froth forms soft peaks.

3 Gradually add the sugar, a tablespoon at a time while continuing to whisk fast, until a stiff meringue is formed.

4 Fill a piping bag, fitted with a ½in (12mm) star nozzle, with meringue mixture. Pipe out eight oval-shaped bases, 2½in (6cm) long, with a rim around each to form a shallow nest for the body of the swan. Also pipe out eight S-shaped scrolls, 2in (5cm) long, to form the swan's neck and head.

5 Bake for 2-3 hours until the meringue is crisp. Leave the oven door slightly ajar if the meringue starts to brown. Allow to cool on the tray.

6 Just before serving, assemble the swans. Whip the cream until it forms stiff peaks and fill a piping bag fitted with ½in (12mm) star nozzle. Pipe a generous swirl of cream into the centre of the 'body' base. Embed the base of a 'neck' into the cream at one end.

7 Cut each pineapple slice in half – or quarters, depending on the diameter of the pineapple – and push one piece into either side of the cream to form the swan's wings. Arrange thin slices of strawberry along the centre of the swan's back for colour and decoration.

8 It is important to keep the finished swans cool before you serve them. This is because the cream needs to be cool to keep its shape. Serve at a tea party or as a dessert, on a lake of home-made raspberry purée.

5 Bake for 2-3 hours until the rounds are dry and crisp. If the meringue seems to be colouring up, leave the oven door slightly ajar.

6 Out of the oven, allow to cool completely before gently easing the rounds off the paper.

7 Whip the cream until it forms stiff peaks. Place one meringue round on a flat serving dish and spread some of the whipped cream over it. Arrange a third of the nectarine slices around rather than across the top.

8 Spread a little cream over a second meringue round's base before pressing it gently over the nectarine slices. Cover with more cream and nectarines. Then spread the base of the third meringue disc with cream and position as the top tier of the gateau.

9 Arrange the rest of the nectarine slices radially from the centre, and spoon small blobs of whipped cream around the rim. Chill until ready to serve.

Baked Alaska

You will need
◇ 1 sponge cake – 8in (20cm) in diameter – or trifle sponges to cover the base of a 9in (23cm) ovenproof plate or flan dish
◇ 2tbsp fresh orange juice or 2tbsp Grand Marnier liqueur
◇ 1 punnet strawberries, sliced
◇ 6 large scoops of vanilla or raspberry ripple ice cream
◇ 3 egg whites
◇ 6oz (180g) powdered sugar

1 Place the sponge cake on an ovenproof plate that is about 2in (5cm) bigger in diameter than the cake.

2 Sprinkle the orange juice or liqueur over the sponge to moisten it slightly. Arrange the strawberry slices on top.

3 Pile the scoops of ice cream on top of the fruit and place in the freezer until you are ready to make the meringue.

4 Heat the oven to 220°C (425°F; Gas 7). Whisk the egg whites until they form soft peaks. Gradually add the sugar, a tablespoon at a time, whisking constantly, to form a stiff meringue.

5 Take the ice-cream base out of the freezer and spread the meringue all over it, taking great care to make sure that the ice cream is completely sealed. Bake for 3-5 minutes until the peaks of the meringue are just tinged brown.

6 Serve as soon as it is taken out of the oven, so that the ice cream has no chance to melt.

Mocha iced meringue cake

You will need
◇ 6 egg whites
◇ 12oz (360g) powdered sugar
◇ 1tsp instant coffee dissolved in 1tsp of hot water
◇ 2pt (1 litre) good chocolate ice cream
◇ 16fl oz (500ml) whipping cream
◇ 2tbsp Tia Maria coffee liqueur
◇ 2oz (60g) flaked almonds, toasted

1 Heat the oven to 110°C (225°F; Gas ¼). Line three baking trays with silicone non-stick baking parchment. Mark 8in (20cm) circles on each tray, using a plate as a guide.

2 Prepare the meringue following the instructions in steps 2 and 3 of the nectarine meringue gateau, adding the coffee with the last of the sugar, and continue to whisk the mixture.

3 Divide the meringue equally between the three marked circles and spread out into flat discs with a palette knife.

4 Bake for 2-3 hours until the rounds are dry and crisp. Leave to cool and then place in the freezer for 30 minutes before assembling the gateau. At the same time, transfer half of the chocolate ice cream to the fridge to soften slightly.

5 After half an hour, take one of the meringue discs from the freezer and place it on a freezer-proof serving plate. Spread the softened ice cream over the top, place another disc of meringue on top and return to the freezer for 30 minutes. At the same time, put the remaining ice cream in the fridge to soften as before.

6 After 30 minutes, take the partially assembled cake from the freezer and spread the rest of the softened ice cream on top. Cover with the remaining disc of meringue and return to the freezer to firm up

7 Meanwhile, pour the cream and Tia Maria liqueur into a mixing bowl and whip until it forms stiff peaks. Take the cake out of the freezer and spread the cream all over it, smoothing out with a palette knife. Top with the almonds and return to the freezer until nearly ready to serve.

8 Leave the cake to stand at room temperature for about 10 minutes to make it easier to slice. Dipping the knife in hot water before cutting will also help to slice through the icy layers more easily. As a special treat, serve each slice on a pool of chocolate sauce.

▽ *Baked Alaska.*

Puff pastry

*Few foods tempt the palate quite like puff
pastries filled with deliciously rich cream and topped with
melted chocolate, caramel sauce or spun toffee.
Stack individual puff pastries into a pyramid, or simply pile
them on to a platter – and spoil your guests.*

When choux paste is put in the oven, it will puff up to twice its original size because of the high proportion of eggs in the mixture. The cooked pastry is fluffy and light – it makes a perfect case for sweet, creamy fillings or adventurous savoury sauces.

Perfect results
Despite its impressive appearance, puff pastry is not difficult to make, provided these simple guidelines are followed:
◇ Add the flour all at once and beat until the mixture forms a thick ball of dough. If it is too soft, place the pan over a gentle heat to stiffen the consistency of the dough.
◇ Preheat the oven to the correct temperature before cooking the paste or it will not rise properly.
◇ Always slit the pastry open after baking. This allows steam to escape and prevents a soggy texture.
◇ Do not fill the pastries too far in advance or they may loose their crispness.

Choux pastry
Basic choux paste mix is used for profiteroles, éclairs and almond rings as well as savoury dishes.

You will need
◇ 2½oz (65g) plain flour
◇ 2oz (50g) butter
◇ 2 eggs, beaten
◇ Optional: for chocolate-flavoured pastry, substitute ½oz (15g) sifted cocoa powder for ½oz (15g) of flour

1 Sift the flour and put to one side. Place the butter in a saucepan with ¼pt (150ml) water. Heat until butter has melted. Bring to the boil and remove from the heat. Immediately tip in flour and beat with a wooden spoon until mixture forms a dough that leaves the sides of the pan cleanly. Cool for two minutes.

2 Gradually add the beaten egg to the mixture, beating well. Continue beating until mixture is glossy and just holds its shape. If the paste is not going to be used immediately, cover pan with a sheet of dampened greaseproof paper and put the lid on top.

Shaping choux paste
Use a quantity of the basic choux mix to make a selection of pastries. Before shaping the paste, preheat the oven to 220°C (425°F; Gas 7). Then fit the chosen nozzle into a piping bag and fill with the paste mixture. If you do not have a piping bag, carefully spoon the mixture on to the tray.

Baking choux paste
1 Cook paste in a preheated oven for 20-25 minutes, or until it has risen and looks crisp and golden.

2 Using a sharp knife, make a slit down long side of éclairs to let steam escape. For buns or profiteroles cut down one side. Cut rings in two horizontally.

△ *Individual puff pastries make a perfect tea-time treat. The one basic mixture can be used to make a range of pastries as shown here, from chocolate-topped éclairs, cream-filled profiteroles topped with either toffee or chocolate to almond-cream rings.*

Filling puff pastries
For all the pastries, sweeten heavy or whipping cream with a little confectioner's sugar and flavour it with brandy or a liqueur.

Place the flavoured, whipped cream in a piping bag fitted with a star nozzle. Open out pastry slightly and pipe cream into the centre. For puff pastry rings, sandwich the two halves together with cream.

Eclairs

Eclairs – fingers of puff pastry, filled with cream and coated with chocolate or coffee-flavoured icing – are definitely irresistible.

You will need
◇ Quantity basic choux paste mix
◇ Plain nozzle, about ½in (lcm) in diameter
◇ Star nozzle about ¾in (2cm) in diameter
◇ Large nylon piping bag
◇ Large baking sheet, lightly greased
◇ Whipped cream (see 'Filling puff pastries')
◇ Melted dark chocolate or glacé icing, flavoured with a little coffee essence or strong black coffee

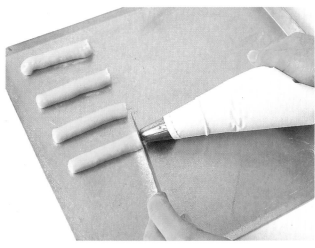

1 Using the plain nozzle, pipe 3in (7.5cm) lengths of paste on to the lightly greased baking sheet. Use a wet knife to cut off the paste next to the nozzle. Space the éclairs well apart to allow room for them to expand while cooking. Bake as given.

2 Make a deep cut lengthways into the éclair using a sharp knife. Fit the star-shaped nozzle to a piping bag and fill bag with the prepared cream. Pipe cream into centre of éclair.

3 Coat the top of some éclairs with melted chocolate. For variety, coat the remainder with coffee-flavoured icing.

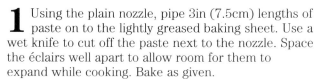

Almond rings

Flaked almonds, sprinkled on to a ring of uncooked choux paste, toast to perfection while the pastry is cooking. Sandwich the rings together with liqueur-flavoured cream. A light dusting of confectioner's sugar completes the topping for this tasty tea-time treat.

You will need
◇ Quantity basic choux paste mix
◇ Plain and star-shaped nozzles and piping bag as for éclairs
◇ Whipped cream
◇ Flaked almonds
◇ Confectioner's sugar
◇ Large baking sheet, lightly greased

1 Using the plain nozzle, pipe rings 3in (7.5cm) in diameter on to baking sheet. Sprinkle rings with flaked almonds. Bake as given.

2 Using a sharp knife, cut the rings in half horizontally. Fit the star-shaped nozzle to piping bag and sandwich the pastry rings together with piped cream. Dust the top lightly with confectioner's sugar.

◆ TIP	STORING

Choux paste can be cooked in advance and stored in an airtight container for several days. Alternatively, freeze in polythene bags for up to three months. To defrost, place frozen paste in a moderate oven for 5-10 minutes to crisp up.

Profiteroles

Profiteroles can be served in many ways. Top individual profiteroles with melted chocolate or coffee-flavoured icing and fill them with cream. Pile a number into a dessert bowl and pour melted chocolate over them just before serving or, to make a spectacular dessert, stack cream-filled profiteroles into a large pyramid and top them with a chocolate or caramel sauce.

Individual profiteroles

The paste for profiteroles can be piped with either a plain or a star-shaped nozzle. Fill pastries with cream, custard or chocolate cream.

You will need
◇ Quantity basic choux paste mix
◇ Whipped cream (see Filling puff pastries, page 112)
◇ Icing, chocolate or caramel sauce (see below) for topping
◇ Plain and star nozzles as described for eclairs
◇ Large nylon piping bag
◇ Large baking sheet, lightly greased

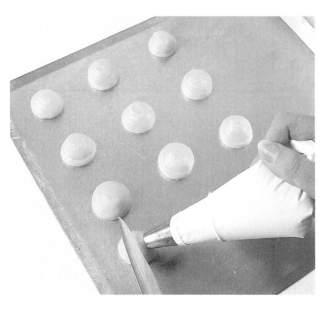

1 Using the plain nozzle, pipe portions about 1in (2.5cm) across on to the baking sheet. Use a wet knife to cut off the pastry next to the nozzle. Buns are shaped in the same way by piping larger portions up to 2in (5cm) across.

2 Alternatively, for star-shaped profiteroles use the star nozzle to pipe portions about 1in (2.5cm) across on to the baking sheet.

3 Bake as given. Either slice into the profiterole with a knife and then pipe cream into the centre, or use a piping bag fitted with a finer nozzle to 'inject' the profiterole with cream. Top with icing, caramel sauce or melted chocolate as desired.

Caramel choux pyramid

For a really impressive dessert, make a pyramid of cream-filled profiteroles topped with caramel. For extra interest, flavour half the profiteroles with chocolate (see the basic choux paste recipe on page 111). Spun toffee, as shown on page 111, is often used to add a lavish touch to a pyramid.

You will need
◇ 1 batch plain profiteroles, filled with cream
◇ 1 batch chocolate-flavoured profiteroles, filled with cream
◇ 8oz (225g) powdered sugar

1 To make the caramel syrup, fill a small, heavy-based saucepan with ¼pt (150ml) water and gradually add the powdered sugar. Stir continuously until all the sugar is dissolved. Bring water and sugar mixture to the boil and simmer until the mixture is a pale golden colour. Remove from heat and immediately put the base of the saucepan in a bowl of cold water to prevent the caramel from cooking further.

2 Carefully dip one side of each profiterole in the syrup. Arrange profiteroles in a circle on a serving plate. Use the caramel to secure the pastries together. If the caramel sets in the pan before you have finished, re-melt over a gentle heat.

3 Fill the centre of the circle of pastries with more profiteroles. Working as quickly as possible, add more layers of pastries over the first, building up a pyramid shape.

Caramel cakes

Caramelized sugar makes one of the most delicious finishes for cakes. It may be mixed with nuts for praline, spun into 'angels' hair', or set in a sheet to top a cake. However you choose to use it, caramel is a fine embellishment for all kinds of pâtisserie.

Caramel nut gâteau

You will need
◇ Two 8in (20cm) plain sandwich sponges
◇ Butter for greasing
◇ 8oz (225g) powdered sugar
◇ 5 tbsp water
◇ 8 whole hazelnuts
◇ 3 tbsp brandy
◇ ¾pt (450ml) whipping cream
◇ 2oz (50g) hazelnuts, chopped

1 Butter a baking tray and line it with greaseproof paper. Butter the inside of an 8in (20cm) flan ring and set it on the greaseproof paper.

2 To make the caramel, put the powdered sugar and water in a small saucepan and stir over a low heat until the sugar is completely dissolved.

3 Then bring the mixture to the boil and cook without stirring until the syrup turns a golden brown. Reserving 2 tablespoons, pour the rest immediately into the flan ring, spreading it right to the edges.

4 Quickly dip the whole nuts in the reserved syrup. Place them on the greaseproof paper and leave to cool. As soon as the caramel disc begins to set, mark it into 8 segments with a knife. Leave to cool and harden.

5 Add the brandy to the caramel saucepan. Cover and warm over a low heat to dissolve the syrup sticking to the pan. Remove and cool by setting the pan in cold water.

6 Whip the cream to soft peaks. Put 5oz (150g) into a piping bag fitted with a ½in (1cm) rose nozzle.

7 Gradually whip the brandy liquid into the remaining cream to a spreading consistency. Use about half to sandwich the cakes and spread the rest around the sides. Coat the sides with chopped nuts.

8 Remove the flan ring from the caramel with the tip of a sharp knife. Use two fish slices to slide the whole disc on top of the cake. Pipe a rosette of cream on each segment and top each with a glazed nut. Serve within 1 hour.

▽ *Caramel nut gâteau.*

Nut torte

This cake is made like a whisked sponge but it contains ground nuts instead of flour and has a crisp caramel topping instead of frosting. You can use walnuts, almonds, hazel, cashews or a mixture of nuts.

If you are not planning to serve the torte until the following day, it is advisable to delay making the caramel until then because it absorbs moisture from the air and loses its crispness.

You will need

◇ 2oz (50g) unblanched ground almonds,
◇ 2oz (50g) ground walnuts
◇ 4 eggs, separated
◇ 5oz (150g) powdered sugar
◇ Oil for greasing

For mocha buttercream

◇ 1 teaspoon instant coffee
◇ 2 teaspoons cocoa powder
◇ 3oz (75g) confectioner's sugar
◇ 2oz (50g) unsalted butter

For caramel topping

◇ 3oz (75g) granulated sugar
◇ 3 tablespoons water
◇ 1oz (25g) walnut halves

1 Heat the oven to 180°C (350°F; Gas 4). Grease and line two 7in (18cm) sandwich tins.

2 Whisk together the egg yolks and powdered sugar until pale and thick.

3 Whisk the egg whites to stiff peaks. Using a metal spoon, fold the whites and ground nuts gently into the egg yolk mixture. Pour into the sandwich tins and level off. Bake for 30 minutes or until the top springs back when gently pressed.

4 Remove from the oven and allow to stand for 30 minutes before turning out on to a wire rack to cool.

5 Meanwhile, make the mocha buttercream. Sift the coffee, cocoa powder and confectioner's sugar into a bowl.

6 Cream the butter and then gradually stir in the coffee, cocoa and confectioner's sugar mixture until smooth.

7 When the sponge is cold, place one layer on a serving plate. Spread with the mocha buttercream and top with the other layer.

8 Make the caramel topping by stirring the sugar and water in a saucepan over a low heat until completely dissolved. Increase the heat and boil without stirring until the syrup caramelizes, about 6-8 minutes. Remove from the heat.

9 Pour the caramel on top of the torte, spreading it with an oiled palette knife neatly to the edge. Arrange the walnut halves on top quickly before the caramel hardens. Press the back of a knife into the caramel, marking it into 8 portions to make it easier to cut when serving.

10 When the remaining caramel in the pan has cooled slightly, dip the prongs of a fork in it, draw it up in threads and trickle over the nuts.

▽ *Nut torte.*

Cakes with cream

*Whipped cream is the ideal complement to most types of cake.
It can be used plain or flavoured with liqueurs, chocolate or vanilla sugar,
as a filling or spread and piped for delicious decoration.*

Strawberry ice gâteau

You will need
◇ 6oz (175g) butter
◇ 6oz (175g) powdered sugar
◇ 3 eggs
◇ 6oz (175g) self-raising flour
  For the decoration
◇ 4oz (125g) plain chocolate
◇ 6oz (175g) strawberries
◇ ¼pt (150ml) whipping cream
◇ A family-sized brick of
  strawberry ice cream

1 Heat the oven to 190°C (375°F; Gas 5). Grease and line two 9in (23cm) sandwich tins.

2 Cream together the butter and sugar until pale and fluffy. Beat in the eggs, one at a time, adding a tablespoon of flour if the mixture begins to curdle. Then fold in the remaining flour.

3 Divide the mixture between the tins and bake for 30 minutes or until the top springs back when gently pressed. Turn out on to a rack to cool.

4 Grate the chocolate. Keeping back 1oz (25g), melt the rest in a bowl over a pan of hot water.

5 Make 5 cones of silicone paper, coat the insides with the melted chocolate and allow to set. Remove the paper when the chocolate is firm.

6 30 minutes before serving, slice the strawberries. Keep a few for decoration. Whip the cream to soft peaks.

▽ *Strawberry ice gâteau, an impressive yet simply made cake.*

1 Heat the oven to 190°C (375°F; Gas 5). Grease and line two 9in (23cm) round sandwich tins.

2 Cream together the butter and sugar until light and fluffy. Beat in the eggs, one at a time.

3 Fold in the flour and the salt, using a large metal spoon. Stir in a little hot water to give a soft dropping consistency.

4 Divide the mixture evenly between the tins and smooth the surfaces. Bake for 20-25 minutes until golden brown and springy to the touch.

5 Turn the cakes on to a wire rack, carefully remove the lining papers, and leave to cool completely.

6 Meanwhile, make the filling. Beat together the softened butter and confectioner's sugar until smooth. Blend the cocoa powder with ½ tablespoon of hot water and add to the mixture. Beat until smooth and evenly blended.

7 Reserve 40 cherries for the topping and roughly chop the remainder. Add the chopped cherries to the buttercream and mix well.

8 Spread one sponge layer with the buttercream mixture and put the other one on top.

9 Whip the cream until stiff. Spread half of it over the top and sides of the gateau. Then coat the sides with the grated chocolate, reserving a little for the top.

10 Place the remaining cream in a piping bag fitted with a large star nozzle and pipe a decorative border around the cake. Arrange the reserved cherries inside the border. Pipe the remaining cream into swirls or rosettes in the centre of the gateau and sprinkle with the remaining grated chocolate. Chill until ready to serve.

△ *Black cherry gâteau.*

7 Place one layer of sponge on a serving plate. Lay slices of the ice cream on it and arrange the sliced strawberries over the top. Put the second sponge cake on top and press gently together.

8 Cover the top and sides with two-thirds of the cream and press the reserved grated chocolate around the sides.

9 Put the remaining cream into a piping bag fitted with a rose nozzle. Pipe the cream into the chocolate cones and place on top of the cake. Lay the reserved strawberries on top and pipe rosettes in the centre. Serve immediately.

Black cherry gâteau

You will need
- 8oz (225g) butter
- 8oz (225g) powdered sugar
- 4 eggs
- 8oz (225g) self-raising flour, sifted
- A pinch of salt
- Butter for greasing

  For the filling
- 2oz (50g) butter, softened
- 4oz (125g) confectioner's sugar
- 2tbsp cocoa powder

  For the topping
- 6oz (454g) can pitted black cherries, drained
- 15 fl oz (426ml) whipping cream
- 12oz (40g) plain chocolate, grated

Crème Chantilly

The smooth, sweet taste of crème Chantilly complements a range of sweets — from melt-in-your-mouth profiteroles to simple confections of fruit. Add a sinful dash of your favourite liqueur, or fold fresh fruit through the cream for a lavish touch.

Making perfectly whipped cream is an art that is well worth mastering! The crème Chantilly described here is really little more than cream sweetened with sugar, yet to achieve just the right consistency these simple guidelines must be followed.

Always beat the cream while it is cold, in a bowl placed in ice. This chill increases the volume and lightness of the cream. Whip the cream until it just holds its shape — over beating will completely ruin the cream, eventually making butter.

You will need
◇ ¹/₂pt (300ml) heavy cream
◇ 25g (1oz) confectioner's sugar, sifted
◇ 1 vanilla pod
◇ Two mixing bowls
◇ Crushed ice
◇ Whisk

1 Fill the large bowl with crushed ice and place the smaller bowl on top.

2 Pour the heavy cream into the small bowl and whisk quickly, making sure that you scrape the cream from the sides of the bowl as you whisk.

3 When the cream is beaten to an airy consistency, open the vanilla pod lengthways with a sharp knife, push out the seeds and add to cream. Pour in the sifted confectioner's sugar.

4 Continue to beat in an energetic, circular motion until the cream has a firm texture and forms peaks when lifted up.

5 Refrigerate until ready for use. If using fruit, fold this into cream just before serving. Fold in liqueur (optional) before piping or serving cream.

◆ TIP	EGG WHITES

For an extra light, fluffy cream fold the stiffly beaten white of one egg into the whipped cream. This makes a luscious filling for cakes.

◁ *Cream to be piped needs a firmer texture, so add extra confectioner's sugar to the basic recipe.*

Cheesecakes

Cool and creamy, rich but tangy, cheesecakes always make popular desserts. With a fresh fruity topping, they make a very attractive sweet to serve to a group of family or friends at a buffet lunch or dinner.

Most cheesecake recipes are designed to serve at least eight to ten people, which again makes them ideal party food. They can be prepared well in advance, as long as they are kept cool in the fridge until you are ready to serve them.

There are basically two kinds of cheesecake, those that are baked to firmness and the ones that are firmed up with a setting agent such as powdered gelatine – agar-agar for

vegetarians – or flavoured jelly. When mixing either filling, you can substitute low-fat cream cheese for the full-fat variety to ensure that it is not highly calorific.

Crushed graham crackers make perfect bases for all kinds of cheesecakes. If you like a hint of chocolate in the base, substitute some chocolate cookies for the plain ones. Use a food processor to pulverize the cookies, or put them in a strong plastic bag and crush them to crumbs with a rolling pin.

Cheesecakes are distinguished by their toppings and decorations. The juiciness and vibrant colours of fresh nectarines, strawberries and

△ *Baked soured cream cheesecake.*

raspberries go very well with the cheesecake mixture. When fresh soft-fruits are out of season, you will find tinned or bottled black cherries, blueberries or blackcurrants make delicious alternatives with strong flavours and colours. Simply thicken the juice slightly with a little arrowroot to give it a gloss.

For a more sophisticated, alcoholic taste, you can flavour the cheesecake mixture with some raisins soaked in a tablespoon or two of rum. Chocolate and cream cheese, too, form a very rich, compatible partnership.

Baked soured cream cheesecake

You will need
For the base
◇ 2oz (60g) butter, melted
◇ 4oz (120g) graham crackers, crushed
◇ 4tsp ground cinnamon
For the filling
◇ 1lb (480g) cream cheese
◇ 4oz (120g) powdered sugar
◇ 3 eggs, beaten
◇ Grated rind of 1 lemon
◇ 2tsp lemon juice
◇ 1tsp vanilla essence
For the topping
◇ 10fl oz (300ml) soured cream
◇ 1oz (30g) powdered sugar
◇ 2tsp vanilla essence
◇ Grated lemon and lime rind

1 Heat the oven to 180°C (350°F; Gas 4). Mix together the melted butter, cookie crumbs and cinnamon. Press into the base of a greased loose-bottomed 8in (20cm) cake tin. Bake for 10 minutes.

2 To make the filling, beat together the cream cheese and sugar. When well mixed, gradually beat in the eggs. Stir in the lemon rind, lemon juice and vanilla essence.

3 Pour on top of the base in the cake tin and bake for an hour or until the centre is firm to the touch. Remove from the oven and increase the temperature to 230°C (450°F; Gas 8).

4 Mix together the ingredients for the topping and spread over the top of the cheesecake. Bake for 8 minutes until set. Remove from the oven and cool in the tin to room temperature. Carefully remove from the tin and chill until ready to serve.

5 Before serving, decorate around the rim of the cheese-cake with finely grated strips of lemon and lime zest.

Nectarine cheesecake

You will need
◇ 5oz (150g) graham crackers, crushed
◇ 2oz (60g) butter, melted
◇ 4¾oz (140g) packet peach or lemon jello
◇ 5fl oz (150ml) hot water
◇ 12oz (360g) full-fat soft cheese, softened
◇ 4 ripe nectarines, stoned
◇ 5fl oz (150ml) whipping cream, whipped
◇ Sprigs of mint to decorate

1 Combine the cookie crumbs and butter thoroughly. Press into the base of a greased loose-bottomed 8in (20cm) cake tin. Chill for 30 minutes until firm.

2 Dissolve the jello in the hot water, cool, then gradually stir in the cheese. Add 2 skinned and chopped nectarines. Fold in whipped cream.

3 Pour into the tin, on top of the chilled base, levelling off the top with a spatula. Chill in the refrig-erator until set. Remove from the tin and decorate with slices of the remaining fruit and arrange small sprigs of mint around the rim.

Variation on a theme

For an exciting orange and chocolate variation on the baked cheesecake, make up the recipe as described, using the grated rind and juice of an orange rather than a lemon. Remove from the oven at step 3 and allow to cool. Peel two oranges, cut out the segments and arrange radially round the edge of the cooled cheesecake. Melt 4oz (120g) of chocolate in a bowl over hot water and pour over the top of the cheesecake so that it just covers the surface and inner tips of the orange segments.

▽ *Nectarine cheesecake.*

Ice-cream bombes

Layered ice-cream bombes are a spectacular way to present shop-bought ice cream. Mix the ice cream in flavours and colours of your choice and add lavish decorations for a special occasion, or leave the smooth outer layer untouched for a simpler look.

Ice-cream bombes are made by layering a selection of flavoured ice creams or sorbets in a special metal mould. Once frozen solid, the bombe can be removed from the mould and kept in a freezer until it is to be decorated and served. The key to success lies in allowing enough time for each layer of the bombe to fully set before adding the next one.

△ *Despite their spectacular appearance, ice-cream bombes are surprisingly easy to make from shop-bought or home-made ice cream, sorbets and fruits.*

Shop-bought or home-made ice cream may be used in a bombe, but it must be of good quality with a smooth and creamy texture. Avoid cheaper varieties of ice cream which can taste synthetic and may fail to set hard enough if they have been over-aerated.

Instead of buying several different flavours of ice cream, you could opt for a rich, creamy vanilla and simply beat in the flavourings of your choice, such as nuts, chocolate, coffee, crushed fruit or mint (see pistachio and raspberry bombe below). For a special occasion, add a few drops of liqueur to the ice cream, such as brandy, Cointreau or Grand Marnier.

The finished bombe should be kept in the freezer ready to transfer to the fridge half an hour before serving; this will soften the bombe for easy slicing, but will not allow it to melt.

Materials and equipment

An ice-cream bombe mould, available from large kitchenware shops, is the only specialist piece of equipment needed to make the bombes. Bombe moulds are made of metal and are generally sold with lids for easy storage of the finished bombe. Different sizes are available with shapes varying slightly from fairly shallow, hemispherical moulds to deeper moulds, the sides of which are almost vertical.

A practical alternative to the shallower type of ice-cream mould is a glass mixing bowl with a capacity of about 2-3 pints (1-1.6l). The technique is exactly the same whichever type of mould you decide to use.

Pistachio and raspberry bombe

The prettiest and most appetising bombes combine a delicious mixture of flavours with an eye-catching array of colours — like this vanilla, pistachio and raspberry sorbet bombe. Sorbets add a light, refreshing touch to thick, rich ice cream. Because of their lighter texture, the sorbets are best placed at the centre of the bombe rather than on the outside or between two layers of ice cream. The bombe is finished with delicately piped chocolate 'lace' end a colourful ring of bright summer fruits, such as strawberries, raspberries and redcurrants.

You will need

◇ Ice-cream bombe mould
◇ Mixing bowls
◇ Sharp knife
◇ 2½pts (1.4l) good quality vanilla ice cream
◇ 4oz (100g) shelled pistachio nuts
◇ ½tsp almond essence
◇ ½pt (300ml) raspberry sorbet
◇ 4oz (100g) fresh or frozen raspberries
◇ 4oz (100g) plain chocolate to decorate
◇ Piping bag fitted with fine writer nozzle

TIP	ICE CREAM

◇ If ice cream slips around mould or bowl when adding first layer, replace mould in freezer for a while. Always return bombe to freezer if it becomes soft while layering ice creams.

◇ If the bombe is too cold to handle, protect your hands with a tea-towel or oven gloves.

1 Place approximately 1¾pt (950ml) of the vanilla ice cream in the mixing bowl and return remainder to freezer until needed. Use back of spoon to mash ice cream until soft but not melted. Pack ice cream into mould with spoon, smoothing it over base and up sides to produce an even layer; bring ice cream slightly above rim of mould, as it will shrink back slightly in the freezer. Put in freezer to harden.

2 Place pistachio nuts in a bowl. To loosen skins, cover nuts with boiling water and leave for three minutes. Drain nuts and rub away skins between layers of kitchen paper or tea-towels. Finely chop nuts. Remove remainder of ice cream from freezer and mash to soften. Stir in chopped nuts and almond essence.

3 Remove ice cream mould from freezer and check that vanilla layer has hardened. If it has, spoon in pistachio in an even layer over vanilla, bringing ice cream slightly above rim. Replace in freezer.

4 Roughly chop the raspberries. Remove raspberry sorbet from freezer and mash with back of spoon until soft. Fold in chopped raspberries. Spoon sorbet into centre of ice-cream mould to fill completely and return to freezer to harden.

5 When ice-cream bombe has completely hardened, remove from freezer and use a knife to slice off any ice cream or sorbet that extends above the rim of the mould. Return to freezer.

Removing bombe from mould

Fill a large bowl or basin with very hot water. Remove ice-cream mould from freezer and dip it into water almost up to rim for two or three seconds only. Invert on to a flat serving plate and gently shake mould on plate until it comes away from ice cream cleanly. If ice cream refuses to loosen, dip a cloth in hot water and press around mould as you shake it.

Decorating the bombe

Melt the chocolate and place in a piping bag fitted with a fine writer nozzle. Pipe swirling lines over the ice cream.

Apricot and coconut bombe

This recipe has been made using an ordinary glass mixing bowl rather than a metal bombe mould. However, all the ice-cream bombe recipes can be made in either a bowl or a mould. Here the combination of coconut, apricots, passion-fruit and crunchy cookies gives a light, tangy flavour.

You will need
◇ 2½pts (1.4l) glass mixing bowl
◇ Mixing bowls
◇ Sharp knife
◇ 2pts (1l) good quality vanilla ice cream
◇ ½pt (300ml) passion-fruit sorbet
◇ 8oz (200g) dried apricots
◇ 2tbsp brandy
◇ 1oz (25g) desiccated coconut
◇ Small almond macaroons (ratafia cookies)
◇ Whipped cream to decorate
◇ Toasted almonds to decorate

1 Finely chop the dried apricots and beat them into 1½pts (850ml) of softened vanilla ice cream with the brandy (see step 2 of pistachio bombe). Use a spoon to pack the ice cream into the glass mixing bowl. Smooth it over the base and sides with the back of the spoon in an even layer, remembering to bring the ice cream slightly above the rim of the bowl. Put the bombe in the freezer until completely hardened.

2 Beat desiccated coconut into the remaining soft-ened vanilla ice cream. Remove the bowl from the freezer and check that the apricot ice cream has fully hardened. If it has, press a layer of cookies on to the apricot ice-cream base. Cover the cookies with a layer of coconut ice cream. Then add another layer of cookies and cover this with a layer of passion-fruit sorbet, mak-ing sure the ice cream is packed firmly into mould.

3 Continue to layer ice cream, sorbet and cookies until bowl is filled to just above rim. Return bombe to freezer. Once frozen, remove excess ice cream with knife (see step 5 of pistachio bombe, page 125).

4 Turn bombe out on to serving plate (see page 125) and decorate with piped cream and almonds. Return bombe to freezer.

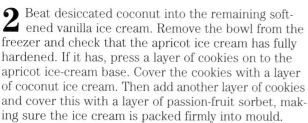

Recipe ideas

Use ice cream of different flavours or add a variety of flavourings to plain vanilla ice cream to create many types of bombes. Decorating the bombes with chocolate, fresh fruits or swirls of piped cream gives a professional final touch.

Chocolate fudge bombe

Line the mould with dark chocolate ice cream, then alternate layers of this flavour and layers of fudge or toffee ice cream. Very thin layers will give an interesting, striped effect when the bombe is sliced.

Fruit sorbet bombe

Use sorbets in contrasting colours, such as lemon, orange, raspberry or strawberry, blackcurrant, kiwi and lime to make a multi-coloured sorbet bombe. Layer the different sorbets to achieve the most dramatic con-trasts of colour.

Coffee and walnut bombe

Beat coffee essence or strong black coffee into vanilla ice cream until it is marbled with colour. Use the coffee ice cream as the outer layer and line with a layer of vanilla ice cream. Finely chop walnuts and stir them into more vanilla ice cream and use this to fill the centre. When the bombe is turned out, decorate with walnut halves.

◁ *Creamy ice cream, tangy sorbet and crunchy cookies are combined in this delicious apricot bombe.*

Index

Page numbers in *italics* refer to photographs

Picture acknowledgements

Photographs: 1 Eaglemoss/Tif Hunter, 4 Eaglemoss/Sue Atkinson, 5 Eaglemoss/Martin Norris, 6 Eaglemoss/Michael Michaels, 7-10 Eaglemoss/Martin Norris, 11 Cent Idées/Duffas/Schoumacher, 12 Eaglemoss/Martin Norris, 13-14 Merehurst Books, 15-17 Eaglemoss/Martin Norris, 18 Merehurst Books, 19-22 Eaglemoss/Martin Norris, 23-24 Eaglemoss/Tif Hunter, 25-26 Eaglemoss/Michael Michaels, 27(t) Eaglemoss/Michael Michaels, (b) Merehurst Books, 28 Eaglemoss/Michael Michaels, 29-42 Eaglemoss/Sue Atkinson, 43 Cent Idées/Duffas/Schoumacher, 44-46 Eaglemoss/Martin Norris, 47-54 Eaglemoss/Sue Atkinson, 55 Eaglemoss/Martin Norris, 56(t) Eaglemoss/Martin Norris, (b) Merehurst Books, 57-58 Eaglemoss/Martin Norris, 59-60 Cent Idées/Duffas/Schoumacher, 61 Eaglemoss/ Sue Atkinson, 62 Cent Idées/Duffas/Schoumacher, 63-67 Eaglemoss/ Sue Atkinson, 68(tr,bl) Merehurst Books, (br) EWA/Di Lewis, 69-72 Eaglemoss/Tif Hunter, 73-80 Eaglemoss/Sue Atkinson, 81 Cent Idées/Duffas/Schoumacher, 82-83 Eaglemoss/Sue Atkinson, 84(t,br) Eaglemoss/Sue Atkinson, (bl) Cent Idées/ Duffas/Schoumacher, 85-88 Cent Idées/Duffas/Schoumacher, 89-106 Eaglemoss/Sue Atkinson, 107 IPC Magazines/Homes and Gardens, 108-110 Octopus Books, 111 National Dairy Council, 112-114 Eaglemoss/Sue Atkinson, 115-118 Octopus Books, 119 National Dairy Council, 120(t,c) Modes et Travaux, (b) National Dairy Council, 121-122 Milk Marketing Board, 123-126 Eaglemoss/Sue Atkinson.

Illustrations: Terry Evans, Coral Mula, Stan North.